**THE NORTO**

Discourse on the Origin of Inequality

**JULIA CONAWAY BONDANELLA** is Professor Emeritus of French and Italian at Indiana University, where she was Associate Dean of the Honors College and taught courses on Italian and Renaissance literature, Western literature and thought, and the history of ideas. She served as Assistant Director of the National Endowment for the Humanities and President of the National Collegiate Honors Council. She is author of *Petrarch's Dream Visions and Their Renaissance Analogues*; co-editor of *The Macmillan Dictionary of Italian Literature*; co-editor and co-translator of *The Italian Renaissance Reader*; and translator and co-editor of *Rousseau's Political Writings*. With Peter Bondanella, she is co-editor and co-translator of Cellini's *My Life* and Machiavelli's *Discourses on Livy* and co-editor of Dante's *Purgatorio* and *Paradiso*.

**FREDERICK NEUHOUSER** has taught philosophy at Harvard University, the University of California, and Cornell University. He is now Professor of Philosophy and Viola Manderfeld Professor of German Language and Literature at Barnard College in New York City. He has written two books on Rousseau: *Rousseau's Critique of Inequality*, a guide to reading the *Discourse on the Origin of Inequality*; and *Rousseau's Theodicy of Self-Love*, on the dangers and redemptive potential of *amour propre*. He is also the author of two books and numerous articles in post-Kantian German philosophy and is Permanent Fellow at the Center for Humanities and Social Change at the Humboldt Universität, Berlin. His current project, inspired by the *Discourse on the Origin of Inequality*, is on what we mean when we call a society "sick."

*For a complete list of titles in the Norton Library, visit*
wwnorton.com/norton-library

**THE NORTON LIBRARY**

# *Jean-Jacques Rousseau*
# Discourse on the Origin of Inequality

*Translated by*

Julia Conaway Bondanella

*Edited by*

Frederick Neuhouser

**W. W. NORTON & COMPANY**
*Independent Publishers Since 1923*

W. W. Norton & Company has been independent since its founding in 1923, when William Warder Norton and Mary D. Herter Norton first published lectures delivered at the People's Institute, the adult education division of New York City's Cooper Union. The firm soon expanded its program beyond the Institute, publishing books by celebrated academics from America and abroad. By midcentury, the two major pillars of Norton's publishing program—trade books and college texts—were firmly established. In the 1950s, the Norton family transferred control of the company to its employees, and today—with a staff of five hundred and hundreds of trade, college, and professional titles published each year—W. W. Norton & Company stands as the largest and oldest publishing house owned wholly by its employees.

Copyright © 2022, 1988 by W. W. Norton & Company, Inc.

Originally published in French as Discours sur l'origine et les fondements de l'inégalité parmi les hommes

All rights reserved
Printed in the United States of America
First Edition

Editor: Pete Simon
Associate Editor: Katie Pak
Editorial Assistant: Olivia Atmore
Project Editor: Maura Gaughan
Compositor: Westchester Publishing Services
Manufacturing by LSC Communications
Book design by Marisa Nakasone and Justin Rose
Production Manager: Karen Romano

Library of Congress Cataloging-in-Publication Data

ISBN: 978-0-393-44124-6 (pbk.)

W. W. Norton & Company, Inc., 500 Fifth Avenue, New York, N.Y. 10110
www.wwnorton.com

W. W. Norton & Company Ltd., 15 Carlisle Street, London W1D 3BS

1  2  3  4  5  6  7  8  9  0

# Contents

# Introduction

Jean-Jacques Rousseau's *Discourse on the Origin of Inequality* is one of the most influential texts in the history of European philosophy. It offers an argument aiming to establish both what makes social inequalities objectionable (when they are) but also where inequality comes from and why it is such a prominent feature of human societies. Rousseau's *Discourse* profoundly influenced the social thought of Adam Smith, Kant, Hegel, Marx, Nietzsche, and many others, but beyond all historical importance, its continuing relevance is difficult to overstate. Although economic inequality is not the only form social inequality takes, it is the easiest to measure, and empirical evidence makes abundantly clear that in poor, developing countries as well as in the richest and most technologically advanced—the United States and the United Kingdom are especially striking examples—disparities between rich and poor are significantly greater now than at any time in the last thirty years. Philosophy may not help much with the gathering of empirical data or in explaining specific examples of the trend just mentioned, but it can attempt to understand why, very generally, inequality is so pervasive and to investigate when, and why, social inequalities become morally objectionable and hence legitimate targets of social critique. This is precisely what the *Discourse on the Origin of Inequality* undertakes to do.

Rousseau was born in 1712 in the politically independent Swiss city of Geneva, the son of a respectable, educated watchmaker and a mother of upper-class origins who died only nine days after giving birth to Jean-Jacques. Although Rousseau ran away from Geneva at the age of fifteen—he sought to escape the beatings of the master to whom he was apprenticed—and only returned twenty-seven years later, the city loomed in both his imagination and his political thought, as demonstrated by his dedication of the *Discourse on the Origin of Inequality* to the "republic of Geneva," which, though considered by many Genevans a model of democratic rule, was in reality a class and gender oligarchy that denied rights of citizenship to the majority of its inhabitants. Rousseau's most famous text, *The Social Contract* (1762), might be thought of as an attempt to imaginatively refashion Geneva, bringing it more into line with its self-professed democratic ideals. Perhaps for this reason, *The Social Contract*, together with his contemporaneous treatise on education, *Emile* (1762), invoked the ire and condemnation of Geneva's Calvinist authorities, and Rousseau spent the last sixteen years of his life in France and Britain fleeing persecution for his supposedly subversive political and religious views. Although he worked prodigiously until the end, his last years were marked by relative isolation, financial insecurity, failing health, and (according to some) paranoia, a plausible consequence of the real persecution he faced for many years. Rousseau died of a stroke in 1778 in the French town of Ermenonville, leaving behind his beloved Thérèse Levasseur, his common-law wife of many years.

Although Rousseau lacked the temperament of a political revolutionary, *The Social Contract* helped to alter the world's political landscape. He inspired the leading figures of the French Revolution to destroy the institutions of feudalism and erect a new social order founded, in theory at least, on principles of equality and individual freedom that had never before been articulated so forcefully. Beyond his political significance, almost every strand of European philosophy that came after him has its origins somewhere in his wide-ranging and unruly corpus. He was not only a philosopher of the first rank, as his contemporaries Hume and Smith recognized, but also an accomplished novelist, essayist, musicologist, autobiographer, botanist, and opera composer. *Julie, or the New Heloise*, his epistolary novel about the conflict between virtue and sexual passion, is said to have been, apart from the Bible, the most widely read book in eighteenth-century Europe. Because of the astounding variety of Rousseau's texts, it is impossible to summarize the main ideas of his thought as a whole—they are too diverse and perhaps too discrepant for that. Yet, a careful reading of his central philosophical works—the *Discourse on the Origin of Inequality*, *The Social Contract*, and *Emile*—reveals a greater systematicity and coherence in his political thought than initial impressions suggest.

The full title of the present text is *Discourse on the Origin and Foundations of Inequality among Men* (1755), but it is often referred to simply as the Second Discourse because it was written not long after another discourse of Rousseau's had appeared, the equally famous *Discourse on the Sciences and Arts* (1751). Both texts were composed as entries in essay-writing competitions sponsored by the royal Academy of Sciences, Arts, and Literature of Dijon.

The First Discourse—which, unlike the Second, won the competition for which it was written—brought Rousseau instant notoriety, in part because of its rhetorical elegance and in part because its central thesis shocked and tantalized his Enlightenment contemporaries: in response to the Academy's question as to whether the restoration of the sciences and arts has contributed to the purification of morals, Rousseau answered with a resounding and unqualified "no," directly contradicting a fundamental assumption of his age, namely, that the cultural advancements of Western European modernity were bound to bring with them moral and political progress as well. It is difficult to find a single, coherent line of argumentation in the First Discourse, but one of its thoughts that exhibits a clear continuity with the Second is that progress in the sciences tends to result in moral corruption because it is fueled by the ambition of those who seek knowledge to be admired for their discoveries and thereby to gain distinction among their peers, with the result that the quest for truth inevitably gets subordinated to the pursuit of praise.

Although it did not win the Academy's prize, the Second Discourse is philosophically, if not necessarily stylistically, superior to the First. One reason is that, contrary to initial impressions, it expounds a complex philosophical position that can be reconstructed in the form of a coherent and compelling argument. A second reason for its superiority is that it expresses more clearly than the First Discourse Rousseau's fundamental *ambivalence* toward "progress" in its various guises. Many readers of the Second Discourse have taken Rousseau to idealize the original state of nature and to prefer it to the modern world because he portrays individuals in that state as independent and happy (or at least free of misery and frustrated desires). Yet, as his important Note IX makes clear, Rousseau does not naïvely prescribe a return to the original state of nature. This is not only because such a return would be impossible but also because he regards it as undesirable. For he takes that primitive condition to be incompatible with the highest aspirations of the human species, which can be achieved only by making use of the various "spiritual" capacities—language, reason, self-consciousness, and love, to mention but a few—available to humans only once they advance beyond their original state of pure but monotonous innocence.

As its full title indicates, the Second Discourse is about both the *origin* and the *foundations* of human inequality, which topics correspond precisely to the two questions proposed by the Academy of Dijon as the subject matter of its competition: What is the origin of inequality among men, and is it authorized by—does it have "foundations" in—natural law? The first of these questions is explanatory in nature, the second normative. That is, the first asks for an account of where human inequality comes from—is it imposed on us by nature, or do we create it ourselves, and, if so, why is it so pervasive?—and the second asks under what conditions, and why, inequality is legitimate, or justified, and under what conditions, and why, it is illegitimate and therefore to be eliminated. One of the difficulties of the Second Discourse is that the position it articulates is more convoluted than the apparent simplicity of its questions leads one to expect. For Rousseau ends up giving surprisingly complex answers to both of his guiding questions.

With regard to the first, he argues that while most inequality is not a direct or necessary consequence of human nature (or of nature more generally), the basic conditions of human *social* existence nevertheless make pernicious forms of inequality—along with many other social ills—difficult to avoid. With regard to the second, he argues that while most familiar forms of social inequality are morally objectionable, they are not bad in themselves but only in virtue of certain undesirable consequences they tend to produce. Moreover, although it is not obvious from the surface of the text, he does not restrict himself to invoking natural law when condemning social inequality. (Indeed, as you will see in his Preface, Rousseau's attitude toward the very concept of natural law is ambivalent.) Instead, in discussing other origins that have been ascribed to political societies in the second half of Part 2, Rousseau implicitly develops a set of criteria for distinguishing legitimate from illegitimate forms of government—the same criteria appealed to later in *The Social Contract*—that also allow him to distinguish acceptable from inacceptable forms of equality, thereby avoiding the simplistic utopian view that social inequality in all its forms is worthy of critique.

A further difficulty posed by the Second Discourse is that even though Rousseau presents it as a genealogy of social inequality, it also investigates the origins of a much wider variety of social ills, including enslavement (or domination), conflict, vice, misery, and self-estrangement. This means that it is often difficult to keep track of how these various phenomena are related, including which are supposed to be the causes of which. Readers encountering Rousseau's text for the first time would do well to approach it with the following simplified schema in mind: the explanatory question of social inequality's origin is primarily (but, of course, not only) a psychological question about where the human impulse to create inequality comes from. This question is pursued alongside another that asks how inequality, once present, is causally related to other social ills—that is, how does inequality result in domination, conflict, vice, misery, and self-estrangement, and how do these phenomena themselves further exacerbate inequality? Finally, untangling these relations provides the key to answering Rousseau's normative question concerning the justifiability of social inequality: to simplify only a bit, social inequalities are illegitimate to the extent that they produce the social ills in question, and they are morally acceptable only when they do not.

Rousseau's explanatory project depends fundamentally on the distinction he draws between two very different forms of self-love that motivate human behavior: on the one hand, "self-love," or *amour propre*—the desire to be esteemed by others—and, on the other, "love of self," or *amour de soi-même*, a natural and benign interest each of us takes in our well-being and preservation. Although it is easy to overlook because of the work's complexity, the Second Discourse repeatedly describes its basic strategy for discovering the origin of human inequality in terms of locating inequality's *psychological* source: "After having proved that inequality is scarcely perceptible in the state of nature . . . , it remains for me to show its origin and progress in the successive developments of the human mind." In light of this, the central explanatory thesis of the Second Discourse can be formulated as the claim that *amour propre* in its inflamed, or corrupted, manifestations—especially when appearing as the desire for *superior* standing in relation to others—explains where social inequality comes from and is the principal source of an array of social ills so widespread that they can seem to be necessary features of the human condition. In making this claim, Rousseau is following both St. Augustine, for whom pride is the source of primal sin, and Hobbes, who regards "glory" as one of the three causes of the state of war that constitutes humankind's natural condition. (Part of the complexity of the *Discourse* is that it takes *amour propre* to be capable of producing the social ills it catalogues only when other, nonpsychological conditions are also present, such as leisure, luxury, the division of labor, private property, and so on. At one point Rousseau describes inflamed *amour propre* as the yeast that fuels the destructive social dynamic described in Part 2 of the *Discourse* but whose leavening power, like that of yeast in the baking of bread, depends on the presence of conditions other than itself.)

Nevertheless, Rousseau's understanding of the role *amour propre* plays in human affairs goes significantly beyond the views of his predecessors. In the first place, he offers a more nuanced account of the many guises an inflamed drive for the esteem of others can take and of the various problems it poses for human well-being. Second, and even more originally, he *suggests* in the Second Discourse (and argues explicitly in *Emile*) that curing these social ills—figuring out how humans can flourish in their communal existence without needing a god to transform their nature—requires not suppressing or overcoming *amour propre* (the attempt at which would be futile or oppressive anyway) but cultivating, or educating, it so that it contributes positively to achieving freedom, peace, virtue, happiness, and unalienated selfhood. The most innovative aspect of Rousseau's position is his claim that, despite its many dangers, *amour propre* is also a condition of nearly everything that gives meaning to human existence and elevates it above that of the beasts. Although the Second Discourse focuses almost exclusively on the dangers of *amour propre*, Rousseau hints even here at the passion's positive potential, for example, in his remark that "it is to this zeal for being talked about, to this frenzy to distinguish ourselves, . . . that we owe what is best and worst among men—our virtues and our vices, our sciences and our errors, our conquerors and our philosophers."

It is not surprising that the healthy forms of *amour propre* that are possible for humans hardly come into view in the Second Discourse itself. For, as Rousseau tells us, its aim is primarily *diagnostic*, namely, to catalogue the principal ills that plague human societies and to explain how they arise and why they are so prevalent: "let us be content [in this discourse] with identifying the evil for which others must supply the remedy." In this context it is important to keep in mind that the Second Discourse articulates only one part of Rousseau's larger philosophical project; *The Social Contract* and *Emile* complement this text by sketching out how just political institutions might be joined with domestic education of the right kind in order to solve the problems diagnosed in the Second Discourse. In this respect the *Discourse on the Origin of Inequality* can be thought of as Rousseau's counterpart to Hobbes's and Locke's accounts of the state of nature, each of which is diagnostic in the sense that it intends to clarify the problems that would plague human social existence in the absence of political institutions and thereby to reveal what problems a just and legitimate political society must solve.

That Rousseau is disputing Hobbes's and Locke's accounts of the state of nature in the Second Discourse is easy to see; it is probably less obvious to contemporary readers that the text is also part of a long tradition of Christian preoccupation with the problem of evil. For, like his theological predecessors, Rousseau undertakes to show here where human evil comes from and how its presence in the world is compatible with the goodness and power of God. Clearly, one of Rousseau's aims is to demonstrate that the source of evil lies not in God, nor in his creation (nature), but in the human will. Locating the cause of the Fall in human freedom is a standard move in Christian theology, and Rousseau's choosing this path, too, is no doubt motivated in part by the traditional theologian's desire to clear God of responsibility for the evil that pervades his creation: if evil enters the world only as the work of human beings, then God and his creation remain faultless. Rousseau gives this familiar idea an important new twist, however, by making human corruption the cumulative and unforeseen result of an extended series of free choices (conjoined with, as Rousseau never tires of pointing out, purely contingent natural occurrences) that, in contrast to the Christian narrative, do not involve the conscious willing of evil. As Rousseau tells the story, neither God nor nature nor the human being bears *moral* blame for the world's corruption. The most for which humans can be reproached is a fateful ignorance of the eventual consequences of their ultimately disastrous though morally innocent choices.

Yet exonerating God is not Rousseau's principal aim in recounting the origin of evil. By offering a naturalistic explanation of human fallenness that invokes neither a sinful human will nor an innate disposition to evil, Rousseau allows for at least the possibility of a this-worldly remedy for human corruption that avoids the need of positing a supernatural power (God's grace) or an otherworldly venue (the life beyond) in order to envisage evil's defeat. Redemption, if it is to occur, can and must be a wholly earthly affair. Rousseau himself points to this possibility in a letter to Voltaire describing the accomplishments of the Second Discourse: "I showed men [there] how they bring their miseries upon themselves, and hence how they might avoid them."[1] In other words, the Second Discourse also has a possible practical function: by pinpointing the source of social ills, it can serve to orient humans' attempts to transform the world so as to eliminate or reduce the pernicious effects of *amour propre* in its corrupted forms.

Finally, the project of the *Discourse*, especially its concern with the extent to which human inequality has its source in nature, can helpfully be compared to classical Greek treatments of the origin and foundations of social inequality. Both Plato and Aristotle ask versions of the same questions, and both respond by arguing that there

---

1. Letter to Voltaire (1756), in Jean-Jacques Rousseau, *The Discourses and Other Early Political Writings*, trans. Victor Gourevitch (Cambridge: Cambridge University Press, 1997), 234.

*is* a basis in nature for human inequality. Since nature endows humans with different capacities and talents that imply a natural hierarchy among them, it qualifies as the principal source, or origin, of inequality. Moreover, this natural inequality is also the normative foundation of social inequalities; it explains why there should be such inequalities and, very generally, who should occupy which positions: actual social inequalities are legitimate—authorized by nature—to the extent that they reflect natural inequalities. For Aristotle there are natural masters and natural slaves, as well as natural differences that justify inequalities between Greeks and barbarians. For Plato there are three types of human souls, each corresponding to a distinct metal: gold, silver, and bronze. For Aristotle these natural differences justify many existing inequalities; for Plato, in contrast, they show the unnaturalness of existing political arrangements and establish the need for radical political reform if society is to be ordered as reason (and nature) demand. For both, thinking of the differences as natural implies that they are not products of human will and that there is nothing humans can or should do to change them.

One of the decisive differences between the classical and modern worlds is that the latter rejects the view that nature legitimizes social inequalities. This move generally goes hand in hand with asserting the fundamental equality, from the point of view of morality, of all human beings. Just what this fundamental equality consists in and what it implies for social philosophy are vexed issues to which modern philosophers give different answers. Yet no matter how these questions are answered, asserting the moral equality of humans poses a problem that the ancients, given their answer to the question of inequality's origin, did not have to face: how can social inequality, a seemingly permanent feature of modern society, be justified if it cannot be traced back to the way that nature set up the world and if there is a prima facie presumption that no one individual has any claim to better treatment by society than any other? Does accepting the moral equality of all humans imply that only a society with no inequalities can be justified?

As noted above, Rousseau argues that inequality does not come from nature (or, more precisely, that nature's contribution to human inequality is so small as to be negligible). For him this means that widespread inequality is not a necessary, invariable feature of human society and that it therefore cannot be justified merely by appealing to the way human beings and their world are naturally constituted. Moreover, if social inequality is a contingent phenomenon that humans introduce into the world, and if its continued presence is up to us, then the question of whether it should exist acquires a significance it lacks if little can be done to alter it. In this sense, the project of the *Discourse on the Origin of Inequality* leads directly into that of *The Social Contract*, which asks precisely under what conditions human society can accommodate a small measure of social inequality while realizing justice by securing the conditions that guarantee the freedom and well-being of all.

—Frederick Neuhouser

# A Note on the Translation

As a process of intensive reading, interpretation, and writing, literary translation requires thoughtful creativity. Every translation is distinctive because linguistic transformations involve invention that goes far beyond the simple transfer of information between languages. An ancient art that has promoted the preservation and dissemination of human thought, literature, and poetry, translation has, over millennia, allowed communication between writers and readers from different ages and people from different linguistic and cultural traditions. From the distant time marked metaphorically by the Tower of Babel, translation has brought to those unable to experience them in the original language insights from writers in all fields of human endeavor. Literary translations have inspired and even served as models for thinkers, writers, musicians, and artists in every era by giving them access to ideas and modes of expression beyond their own traditions. Given the large number of human languages with writing systems, most people would not be able to explore works of great value written in other languages without translation, and valuable cross-fertilizations among civilizations would be lost.

In this context, I have translated Rousseau's *Discourse on the Origin of Inequality*, which offers relevant insights into the thorny debates over the enduring inequalities in human societies. Rousseau's powerful critique of modernity aims to show how natural differences among human beings endowed with certain gifts by their creator, along with the development of social and political institutions, have given rise to inequality. My goal has been to introduce his brilliant analysis of inequality into ongoing contemporary discussions of these issues for those who do not read French. This edition reflects the challenges of the translator's job, which relies on close readings and interpretations that may suggest different solutions. In the case of a philosophical treatise, the translator must also attempt to be an honest conduit for the original, always asking how best to provide an accurate reflection of what the original text is trying to convey, and, with a writer of Rousseau's caliber, paying close attention to style, language, words, and sounds. I hope that this translation gives the English reader some sense of Rousseau's voice, of the power and clarity of his style, of the problematic aspects of his terminology and the ambiguities of his thought. I have tried not to deviate in any significant manner from the original to paraphrase in a personal literary style what I thought Rousseau was trying to say, nor have I attempted to reproduce archaic syntax or diction to create what could only be a false impression of reading an Enlightenment text. I have kept my ear attuned to the style and meaning of the original while creating an appropriate version in the contemporary English that is my idiom. I have tried to make it readable, accessible, and inviting to modern readers. Unlike other modern translators of Rousseau, I have tried to avoid chopping up his sentences by inserting periods, where Rousseau did not intend a full pause and where such a pause would detract from or distort the power of his style and his arguments. My goal as a translator has always been to balance faithfulness to the original with good stylistic practices in English that vary from those in French.

In translating the *Discourse on the Origin of Inequality*, I have attempted to render key terms and concepts in a reasonably consistent fashion, so that the reader can see how they recur and develop in this *Discourse* and Rousseau's other writings. These terms include the following: (1) *Un particulier*, translated as "a private individual," refers to the individual members of a community, whereas the adjective *particulier* is often opposed to *général*, as in the *volonté générale* (general will) and the *volonté particulière* (particular will). I have normally rendered the adjective *particulier* as "particular" to contrast it with *privé* (private), unless the context makes useful the contrast in English between private and public. (2) I draw the distinction between *principe* as a rule of law and *maxime* as a rule of politics by translating the former as "principle" and the latter as "maxim." (3) Rendering the term *convention* as "agreement" avoids the connotation of "conventional" in English, when Rousseau is referring to the legitimate agreements that serve as the cornerstones of a society. Rousseau, however, often opposes the terms *naturel* and *conventionnel*, which I have translated as "natural" and "conventional" or "civil," since the distinction reflects the one Rousseau constantly makes between human beings in the state of nature and those living in civil society. (4) Although any wholly satisfactory equivalents are difficult to find in English, the differences between *amour propre* and *amour de soi-même* are suggested by rather literal translations, respectively "self-love" and "love of self." The latter refers to the individual's natural ability to obtain basic necessities, such as food, drink, and shelter, a basic drive for self-preservation that is one of the gifts bestowed on humankind by the creator. Self-love, a negative passion, defines a new type of self-interest that arises when human beings begin to live in groups, experiencing sexual competition and a growing need to be esteemed by others. (5) I have translated *pitié* as "compassion" to convey Rousseau's idea of a basic drive, a part of our original nature, that pushes us to care for others insofar as it is not detrimental to our self-preservation. (6) To convey the sense of *moeurs* as referring to the manners and morals of a community, I have used the expression "moral habits" to avoid modern sociological terminology, the clumsiness of two nouns, and possible confusion with the translation of *coûtumes* as "customs." (7) The noun *droite* is translated as either "law" or "right," depending upon the context. (8) The word *patrie*, which really has no good equivalent in English but means something like "native country," is rendered as "homeland."

This translation of the *Discourse on the Origin of Inequality* is based on the Pléiade edition of Rousseau's works, specifically upon the *Oeuvres complètes*, volume 3 (Paris: Éditions Gallimard, 2011). I have translated Notes IX, XI, XV, and XIX of those Rousseau appended to the *Discourse*, which provide a first reader with crucial additional arguments.

I am appreciative of all those who have made contributions to this translation, including Alan Ritter and Peter Bondanella. I owe a special debt and much appreciation to Frederick Neuhouser, whose thoughtful reading of the translation contributed in significant ways. I also want to offer sincere thanks to Katie Pak, our editor at Norton, who has, with patience and intelligence, guided the project to its completion.

—Julia Conaway Bondanella

*Jean-Jacques Rousseau*

# Discourse on the Origin
of Inequality

# DISCOURSE

## ON THE

## ORIGIN and FOUNDATIONS

## OF

## Inequality among Men

By JEAN-JACQUES ROUSSEAU,
Citizen of GENEVA

"Non in depravatis, sed in his quae bene secundum
naturam se habent, considerandum est quid sit
naturale."    —ARISTOTLE, *Politics*, I.5.1254a°

# *Preface°*

The most useful and least advanced of all the fields of human knowledge seems to me to be that of man, and I dare say that only the inscription on the temple at Delphi° contained a precept of greater importance and difficulty than all the great tomes of the moralists. Thus, I consider the subject of this discourse to be one of the most interesting questions that philosophy can propose, and, unhappily for us, one of the thorniest that philosophers can try to resolve: For how can the source of inequality among men be known, unless we begin by knowing men themselves? And how will man manage to see himself as nature created him, through all the changes that the passing of time and events must have produced in his original constitution, and to separate what he owes to his own roots from what circumstances and his progress have added to or changed in his original state? Like the statue of Glaucus, which time, sea, and storms had so disfigured that it resembled less a god than a wild beast, the human soul, altered in the midst of society by thousands of constantly recurring causes, by the acquisition of a mass of knowledge and a multitude of errors, by the changes that came about in the constitution of the body, and by the continual impact of the passions, has, so to speak, changed in appearance to the point of being nearly unrecognizable; and instead of a being that always acts according to specific and invariable principles, instead of that celestial and majestic simplicity which its Author imprinted on it, we no longer find anything but the grotesque contrast between passion that believes it is able to reason and understanding in a state of delirium.

What is even more cruel is that, since all the progress made by the human species constantly moves it away from its primitive state, the more we accumulate new knowledge, the more we deprive ourselves of the means of acquiring the most important of all, and, in a sense, it is by virtue of studying man that we have made ourselves incapable of knowing him.

It is easy to see that in these successive changes of the human constitution we must seek the earliest origin of the differences that distinguish men, who, it is agreed, are naturally as equal among themselves as were the animals of each species before various physical causes had introduced in some of them the variety that we now observe. In fact, it is inconceivable that these first changes, by whatever means they came about, altered all at once and in the same manner all the individuals of the species, but while some individuals developed or grew worse, and acquired various qualities, good or bad, that were not inherent in their nature, others remained for a longer time in their original state; such was the first source of inequality among men, so that it is thus easier to give some general indications than to determine its true causes with any precision.

Let my readers not imagine, then, that I dare flatter myself with having seen what appears to me so difficult to see. I began a few lines of argument; I hazarded a few guesses, less with the hope of resolving the question than with the intention of clarifying it and reducing it to its true proportions. Others will easily be able to go farther along this route, without it being easy for anyone to reach the end. For it is no small undertaking to sort out what is original from what is artificial in the present nature of man, and to have a clear understanding of a state that no longer exists, that has, perhaps, never existed, that will probably never exist, and about which it is, however, necessary to have accurate notions in order to judge our own present condition properly.° Anyone who undertakes to determine exactly which precautions to take in order to make solid observations on this subject would need even more philosophy than is generally thought, and a good solution to the following problem would not seem to me unworthy of the Aristotles and Plinys of our century: *"What experiments would be necessary to gain some knowledge of natural man? And what are the means of carrying out these experiments within society?"* Far from undertaking to resolve this problem, I believe that I have meditated sufficiently on the subject to dare respond in advance that the greatest philosophers will not be good enough to direct these experiments, nor the most powerful sovereigns to carry them out; it is scarcely reasonable to expect such cooperation, especially with the perseverance or, rather, the continuity of understanding and good will necessary on every side for success.

These investigations, so difficult to carry out and so seldom thought about until now, are, however, the only means left to us of overcoming a multitude of difficulties that conceal from us the knowledge of the real foundations of human society. It is this ignorance about the nature of man that throws so much uncertainty and obscurity on the true definition of natural right, for the idea of right, says Mr. Burlamaqui, and still more that of natural right, are obviously ideas relating to the nature of man. Therefore, he continues, the principles of this science must be deduced from the very nature of man, his constitution, and his condition.°

It is not without a sense of surprise or shock that we observe how little agreement prevails among the various authors who have treated this important subject. Among the most serious writers we scarcely find two who are of the same opinion on this point. Without speaking of the ancient philosophers, who seem to have made it their business to contradict each other on the most fundamental principles, the Roman jurists indifferently subject man and all the other animals to the same natural law, because they take this term to mean the law that nature imposes on itself, rather than the law that nature prescribes; or rather, because of the particular sense in which those jurists understand the term *law*, which they seem to have taken only as the expression of the general relations established by nature among all living beings for their common preservation. The moderns acknowledge as a law only a rule prescribed to a moral being, that is, a being intelligent, free, and respected in his relations with others, and, consequently, they limit the jurisdiction of natural law to the only animal endowed with reason, that is, to man; but with each one defining this law in his own fashion, they all establish it on such metaphysical principles that even among us few people are in a position to understand these principles, let alone able to discover them on their own, so that all the definitions of these learned men, who are otherwise in perpetual contradiction with each other, agree on this alone, that it is impossible to understand the law of nature and, consequently, to obey it, without being a great thinker and a profound metaphysician, which means precisely that for the establishment of society, men must have made use of the kind of knowledge that is developed only with great difficulty and by very few people within society itself.

Knowing so little of nature and disagreeing over the meaning of the word *law*, it would be very difficult to agree on a good definition of natural law. Thus, all those definitions found in books, aside from a lack of uniformity, also have the flaw of being drawn from several areas of knowledge that men do not naturally possess, and from advantages, the idea of which they cannot even conceive until after having left the state of nature. Writers begin by searching for rules on which it would be useful for men to agree among themselves for the common good; and then they give the name of natural law to this collection of rules, without any other proof than the good that they believe would result from their universal application. Surely this is a very convenient way to compose definitions and to explain the nature of things by virtually arbitrary conventions.

But insofar as we are ignorant of natural man, it will be useless for us to try to determine the law that he received or the one best suited to his constitution. All that we can very clearly see regarding this law is that for it to be law, not only must the will of anyone who is bound by it be capable of submitting to it knowingly, but that, furthermore, for it to be natural, it must speak directly by the voice of nature.

Leaving aside, therefore, all the scientific books that teach us only to see men as they have made themselves, and meditating on the first and simplest operations of the human soul, I believe I perceive in it two principles prior to reason, one of which makes us ardently interested in our well-being and our self-preservation, and the other which inspires in us a natural repugnance to seeing any sentient being, and principally our fellow humans, perish or suffer. It is from the concurrence and combination of these two principles that our mind is capable of creating, without it being necessary to bring into it that of sociability, that all the rules of natural right appear to me to follow, rules that reason is later forced to reestablish on other foundations, when through its successive developments it has ended in stifling nature.

This way, we are not obliged to make man a philosopher before making him a man; his duties toward others are not dictated to him solely by the belated lessons of wisdom, and as long as he does not resist the inner impulse of compassion, he will never do harm to another man, or even to any other sentient being, except in the legitimate case where, since his own preservation is involved, he is obliged to give preference to himself. By this means, we can end the old disputes over the participation of animals in natural law, for it is clear that, bereft of understanding and liberty, they cannot recognize this law, but since they share to some extent in our nature by virtue of the sentience with which they are endowed, it will be concluded that they must also participate in natural right, and that man is subject to some kind of duty toward them. It seems, in fact, that if I am obliged to do no harm to my fellow man, it is less because he is a rational being than because he is a sentient being, a quality common to beast and man that should at least give the former the right not to be needlessly mistreated by the latter.

This same study of original man, his true needs, and the fundamental principles of his duties, is also the only good means that can be used to resolve the host of difficulties that present themselves concerning the origin of moral inequality, the true foundations of the body politic, the reciprocal rights of its members, and a thousand other similar questions that are as important as they are poorly clarified.

Upon considering human society with a tranquil and dispassionate gaze, it seems, at first, to display only the violence of powerful men and the oppression of the weak; the mind rebels against the harshness of the former; it is inclined to deplore the blindness of the latter; and as nothing is less stable among men than those external relationships, more often produced by chance than by wisdom, which are called weakness or power, wealth or poverty, human institutions appear at first glance to be founded on mounds of shifting sand: It is only by examining them closely, only after having cleared away the dust and sand surrounding the edifice, that we perceive the unshakable base on which it has been raised, and that we learn to respect its foundations. Now, without a serious study of man, his natural faculties, and their successive developments, we shall never succeed in making these distinctions, and in separating, in the present constitution of things, what the divine will has done from what human art has pretended to do. The political and moral research inspired by the important question I am examining is therefore useful in every way, and the hypothetical history of governments is, in every respect, an instructive lesson for man. In considering what we would have become, left to ourselves, we should learn to bless Him whose kindly hand, by correcting our institutions and giving them an unshakable foundation, has prevented the disorders that would otherwise result from them, and has brought forth our happiness from means that seemed apt to increase our misery.

> Quem te Deus esse
> Jussit, et humana qua parte locatus es in re,
> Disce.°

# Notice on the Notes[*]

I have added a few notes to this work, according to my lazy custom of working in fits and starts. Sometimes these notes stray so far from the subject that it is not appropriate to read them with the text. I have therefore relegated them to the end of the *Discourse*, in which I have tried my best to follow the straightest path. Those who have the courage to begin again will be able to amuse themselves a second time by beating the bushes and attempting to run through the notes; there will be little harm done if others do not read them at all.

[*] We have included only the most relevant of Rousseau's notes: IX, XI, XV, and XIX, which can be found on p. 87. For the Editor's notes to this Norton Library edition, see Notes, p. 97.

*Question*

Proposed by the Academy of Dijon.

What is the origin of inequality among
men, and is it authorized
by natural law?

# Discourse on the Origin and Foundations of Inequality among Men

It is of man that I am to speak, and the question I am examining tells me that I am going to speak to men, for such questions are not proposed by those who are afraid of honoring the truth. I shall, therefore, defend with confidence the cause of humanity before the wise men who invite me to do so, and I shall not be displeased with myself if I prove myself worthy of my subject and my judges.

I conceive of two kinds of inequality within the human species; one I call natural or physical, because it is established by nature and consists of differences in age, health, bodily strength, and qualities of mind or soul; the other may be called moral or political inequality, because it depends upon a kind of agreement and is established or at least authorized by the consent of men. The latter consists of the different privileges that some enjoy to the detriment of others, such as being more wealthy, more honored, more powerful than they, or even making themselves obeyed by the others.

It is impossible to ask what the source of natural inequality is, because the answer is expressed in the simple definition of the word; it is even more impossible to find out if there is not some essential connection between the two kinds of inequality, for that would amount to asking, in other words, if those who command are necessarily better than those who obey, and if strength of body or mind, wisdom or virtue, are always found in the same individuals in proportion to power or wealth, a good question, perhaps, to be debated among slaves being overheard by their masters, but unsuitable for rational and free men who are seeking the truth.

What precisely is, then, the point of this discourse? To mark in the progression of things, the moment when, right replacing violence, nature was subjected to law; to explain the chain of miracles by which the strong could resolve to serve the weak and the people could purchase a semblance of peace at the price of true felicity.

Philosophers who have examined the foundations of society have all felt the need to go back to the state of nature, but none of them has reached it. Some have not hesitated to attribute the notion of just and unjust to man in that state, without bothering to show that he had to have this notion or even that it was useful to him; others have spoken of the natural right of each to preserve what belongs to him, without explaining what they meant by *belong*. Still others, granting at first the strongest authority over the weakest, have immediately brought forth governments, without considering the time that must have elapsed before the meaning of the words *authority* and *government* could have existed among men. At last, all of them, constantly speaking of need, greed, oppression, desires, and pride, have transported to the state of nature ideas they have acquired in society; they spoke of savage man and they depicted civil man. It has not even entered the minds of most of our philosophers to doubt that the state of nature had existed, whereas it is evident from reading the Holy Scriptures that the first man, having immediately received his knowledge and commandments from God, was not himself in that state, and that in giving Moses's writings the credence that every Christian philosopher owes them, it must be denied that men were ever in the pure state of nature, even before the deluge, unless they fell back into it through some extraordinary circumstance: a paradox highly embarrassing to defend and altogether impossible to prove.

Let us begin, therefore, by dismissing all the facts, for they have no bearing on the question. The research that can be conducted on this subject must not be taken as historical truth, but only as hypothetical and conditional arguments, better suited to shed light on the nature of things than to show their true origin, just like those our physicists make every day about the formation of the world. Religion commands us to believe that since God himself took men out of the state of nature, they are unequal because He wanted them to be so, but it does not forbid us to form conjectures drawn from man's nature alone and from the beings that surround him about what the human race might have become, if it had been left to itself. That is what I am being asked, and what I propose to examine in this discourse. As my subject concerns man in general, I shall try to use a language that suits all nations, or rather, forgetting times and places in order to think only of the men to whom I am speaking, I shall imagine myself in the Lyceum of Athens, repeating the lessons of my masters, with such men as Plato and Xenocrates for judges, and the human race for an audience.

O Man, from whatever country you may come, whatever your opinions may be, listen: here is your history as I have thought I read it, not in the books of your fellow men, which are deceptive, but in nature, which never lies. All that comes from nature will be true; nothing will be false except what I have involuntarily put there on my own. The times of which I am going to speak are very remote: How much you have changed from what you were! It is, so to speak, the life of your species that I am going to describe to you according to the qualities which you have received, that your education and habits have been able to corrupt but not destroy. There is, I feel, an age at which the individual man would like to remain; you shall seek the age at which you would desire your species to have remained. Dissatisfied with your present state, for reasons which promise still greater dissatisfactions for your unfortunate posterity, perhaps you would like to be able to go back, and this sentiment will celebrate your early ancestors, criticize your contemporaries, and terrify those who will have the misfortune to follow you.

## Part 1

However important it may be, in order to assess the natural state of man properly, to consider him from his origin and to examine him, as it were, in the first embryo of the species, I shall not trace its structure through its successive developments; I shall not stop to seek within the animal system what he may have been at the beginning in order to have finally become what he is; I shall not examine whether, as Aristotle thinks, his elongated nails were not at first hooked claws, whether he was not hairy like a bear, and whether, if walking on all fours, his vision, which was directed toward the earth and restricted to a horizon of a few paces, did not reveal both the nature and limits of his ideas. I could make only vague and almost imaginary conjectures on this subject; comparative anatomy has still made too little progress; the observations of the naturalists are still too uncertain for the basis of a sound argument to be established on such foundations. Thus, without having recourse to the supernatural knowledge that we have on this point, and without regard for the changes that must have arisen as much in the internal as in the external conformation of man as he applied his limbs to new uses and fed himself on new foods, I shall suppose him always to have been formed as I see him today, walking on two feet, using his hands as we do ours, casting his glance over all of nature, and measuring with his eyes the vast expanse of heaven.

By stripping this being, thus constituted, of all the supernatural gifts he could have received and of all the artificial faculties he could have acquired only through long progress, by considering him, in a word, as he must have come from the hands of nature, I see an animal less strong than some, less agile than others, but, on the whole, the most advantageously constituted of all; I see him eating his fill under an oak tree, quenching his thirst at the first stream, finding his bed at the foot of the same tree that furnished his meal, with all his needs satisfied.

Left to its natural fertility and covered with immense forests that the axe has never mutilated, the earth offers at every step storehouses and shelter to animals of every species. The men dispersed among them observe and imitate their ingenuity, and thus rise to the level of the instincts of beasts, with the advantage that, unlike any other species which has only its own instinct, man, who has none which belongs to him alone, appropriates them all, lives equally well on most of the different foods that the other animals share, and, consequently, finds his subsistence more easily than any of them can do.

Accustomed from infancy to bad weather and the harshness of the seasons, used to fatigue, and forced, naked and unarmed, to defend their lives and their prey from other wild beasts, or to escape from them by running, men acquire a robust and almost unalterable temperament; children, bringing into the world with them the excellent constitution of their parents and fortifying it by the same exercises that produced it, thus acquire all the vigor of which the human species is capable. Nature treats them precisely as the law of Sparta treated the children of citizens; it makes strong and robust those with sound constitutions and lets all the others perish, differing in that respect from our societies, where the state, by making children burdensome to parents, kills them indiscriminately before their birth.

Since the savage man's body is the only instrument he knows, he puts it to various uses for which our bodies, through lack of exercise, are unfit, and it is our ingenuity that deprives us of the strength and agility that necessity obliges him to acquire. If he had an axe, would he break such strong branches with his hands? If he had a sling, would he throw a stone so hard? If he had a ladder, would he climb a tree so nimbly? If he had a horse, would he be so swift a runner? Give civilized man the time to assemble all these tools around him, and no one can doubt that he will easily overcome savage man, but if you want to see an even more unequal contest, pit them against each other naked and unarmed, and you will soon see the advantage of having all one's strength constantly at one's disposal, of always being ready for every event, and of always carrying one's whole self, so to speak, with one.

Hobbes claims that man is naturally intrepid and seeks only to attack and fight. An illustrious philosopher° thinks, on the contrary, and Cumberland and Pufendorf also assure us, that nothing is as timid as man in the state of nature, and that he is always trembling and ready to flee at the slightest noise he hears or the slightest movement he perceives. That may be so for the things he does not know, and I do not doubt that he is frightened by all the new sights that greet him, whenever he cannot discern the physical good or evil he may expect from them, or compare his strength with the risks that he must run, circumstances rare in the state of nature, where all things function in such a uniform way, and where the face of the earth is not subject to those sudden and continual changes caused by the passions and inconstancy of people gathered together. But savage man, living dispersed among the animals and early on finding himself in a position to measure himself against them, soon makes the comparison, and, sensing that he surpasses them more in agility than they surpass him in strength, he learns to fear them no longer. Pit a bear or a wolf against a savage man, robust, agile, courageous as they all are, armed with stones and a good stick, and you will see that the danger will at the very least be reciprocal, and that after several such experiences, ferocious beasts, which do not like to attack each other, will less willingly attack man, whom they will have found quite as fierce as themselves. With regard to animals that are actually stronger than man is agile, he is, in relation to them, in the position of other weaker species, which do not cease to subsist, with the advantage for man, that being no less fit than they are for running and finding almost certain refuge in trees, he may, in every situation, take or leave any encounter, and make the choice between flight or combat. Let us add that, apparently, no animal naturally makes war upon man except in the case of self-defense or extreme hunger, or shows any of those violent antipathies toward him which seem to indicate that one species is destined by nature to serve as food for the other.

Other, more formidable enemies against which man lacks the same means of defending himself are the natural infirmities, infancy, old age, and illnesses of every kind, sad signs of our weakness, of which the first two are common to all animals, and the last belongs principally to men living in society. I would even observe, on the subject of infancy, that a mother, carrying her child with her everywhere, can feed it much more easily than the females of several animals, which are constantly forced to come and go with great fatigue to seek their food in one place and to suckle and feed their young in another. It is true that if the woman happens to perish, the child runs a strong risk of dying with her; but this danger is common to a hundred other species, whose young are for a long period of time in no position to go seek food for themselves. If infancy lasts longer among us, life also lasts longer, and everything is still nearly equal in this respect, although there are other rules concerning the duration of infancy and the number of young, which are not part of my subject. Among old people, who are less active and perspire little, the need for food diminishes with the ability to provide for it; and since savage life wards off gout and rheumatism, and since old age is, of all ills, the one that human assistance can least alleviate, they finally pass away, without anyone being aware that they are ceasing to exist, and almost without being aware of it themselves.

With respect to illnesses, I shall not repeat the vain and false declamations that most healthy people make against medicine, but I shall ask if there is any solid observation from which it may be concluded that in countries where this art is most neglected the average lifetime of man is shorter than in those where it is cultivated with the greatest care. And how could that be, if we bring upon ourselves more ailments than medicine can furnish remedies! The extreme inequality in our way of living; the excessive idleness of some; the excessive labor of others; the ease of inflaming and satisfying our appetites and our sensuality; the overly refined foods of the rich, which nourish them with juices that overheat and afflict them with indigestion; the bad food of the poor, which they most often lack, so that the deprivation leads them to greedily overburden their stomachs whenever possible; late nights, excesses of every kind, immoderate outbursts of all the

passions, hardships, spiritual exhaustion, countless sorrows and afflictions which are felt in all conditions, and
which perpetually eat at our souls—this is the dreadful
proof that most of our ills are of our own making, and that
we could have avoided nearly all of them by preserving the
simple, unchanging, and solitary way of living which was
prescribed for us by nature. If nature destined us to be
healthy, I almost dare to affirm that the state of reflection
is a state contrary to nature and that the man who med-
itates is a depraved animal. When we think of the good
constitution of savages, at least of those whom we have
not ruined with our strong liquors; when we find out
that they rarely experience any illnesses other than wounds
and old age, we are very much inclined to believe that the
history of human illnesses could easily be written by
following that of civil societies. This is, at least, the opinion of Plato, who judges, on the basis of certain remedies used or approved by Podalirios and Machaon at the
siege of Troy, that the various diseases these remedies
must have inflamed were still not, at that time, known
among men.

    With so few sources of illness, man in the state of
nature has, therefore, scarcely any need of remedies, still
less of physicians; the human species is in no worse a condition, in this regard, than all the others; and it is easy to
learn from hunters whether they find many infirm animals on their hunting trips. They find some which have
suffered substantial injuries that are very well healed,
which have had bones and even limbs broken that have
recovered with no other surgeon than time and no other
regimen than their everyday life, and they are no less
perfectly cured for not having been tormented by inci-
sions, poisoned by drugs, or exhausted by fasting. In short,
however useful properly administered medicine may be
among us, it is always certain that if the ailing savage, left to
himself, has nothing to hope for but from nature, he

has, by contrast, nothing to fear except from his disease, which often makes his situation preferable to ours.

Let us, therefore, take care not to confuse savage man with the men we have before our eyes. Nature treats all the animals left to its care with a partiality that seems to show how jealous it is of this right. The horse, the cat, the bull, even the ass are mostly taller; all have a more robust constitution, more vigor, strength, and courage in the forests than in our homes; they lose half these advantages in becoming domesticated, and it could be said that all our efforts to treat these animals well and to feed them only end up degrading them. This is the case with man himself: In becoming a social being and a slave, he becomes weak, fearful, and servile, and his soft and effeminate way of living ends up completely exhausting both his strength and his courage. Let us add that between the savage and domestic conditions the difference from man to man must be even greater than that from beast to beast, for although the animal and man have been treated alike by nature, man gives himself more conveniences than the animals he domesticates, which are so many specific causes that make him degenerate more visibly.

It is not, therefore, such a great misfortune for these first men, nor is it, above all, such a great obstacle to their preservation, to be nude and to lack shelter, deprived of all those useless things we believe so necessary. If they do not have hairy skin, they have no need for it in warm countries, and, in cold countries, they soon learn how to appropriate the skins of beasts they have defeated; if they have but two feet for running, they have two arms to provide for their defense and their needs; their children perhaps walk late and with difficulty, but the mothers carry them with ease, an advantage lacking in other species, in which the mother, being pursued, is forced to abandon her young or to adjust her pace to theirs. Finally, unless we assume these singular and fortuitous combinations of events, which I shall subsequently discuss and which might very well never occur, it is clear, in any event, that the first person who made himself clothes or lodging thereby gave himself things that were hardly necessary, since he had done without them until then, and since it is difficult to see why he could not have endured as a grown man the kind of life he had endured from his infancy.

Alone, idle, and always a neighbor to danger, savage man must be fond of sleeping, and be a light sleeper, like animals which, thinking little, sleep, so to speak, anytime they are not thinking. Since his own preservation is almost his sole concern, his best-trained faculties must be those that have attack and defense as their main purpose, either to subjugate his prey or to protect himself from being the prey of another animal; organs that are developed only by softness and sensuality, on the contrary, must remain in a crude state, which excludes any kind of delicacy within him, and, since his senses are divided in this way, he will have extremely coarse senses of touch and taste, and sight, hearing, and smell of the greatest subtlety. Such is the condition of animals in general, and it is also, according to the reports of travelers, that of most savage peoples. Thus, we should not be surprised that the Hottentots of the Cape of Good Hope can discover vessels as far out on the high seas with the naked eye as the Dutch with telescopes; or that the savages of America track Spaniards by smell as well as the best dogs; or that all these barbarian nations endure their nakedness easily, stimulate their appetite with red pepper, and drink European liquors like water.

Up to this point, I have considered only physical man; let us now try to look at him from the metaphysical and moral side.

In every animal, I see only an ingenious machine to which nature has given senses to recover and to protect itself, up to a certain point, from all that tends to disturb or to destroy it. I see precisely the same things in the human machine, with the difference that nature alone does everything in the operations of the beast, while instead man contributes to his own as a free agent. The one chooses or rejects by instinct, and the other by a free act, which means that the beast cannot deviate from the rule prescribed for it, even when it would be advantageous to him to do so, and that man often deviates from it to his detriment. That is how a pigeon would die of hunger near a dish of the finest meats, and a cat on a pile of fruit or grain, even though each could very well nourish itself on the food it disdains, if it had only thought of trying some. In this way, dissolute men indulge in excesses, which cause fever and death, because the mind corrupts the senses and the will still speaks when nature is silent.

Every animal has ideas since it has senses; it even combines its ideas up to a certain point, and, in this regard, man differs from beasts only by degree. Some philosophers have even proposed that there is a greater difference between a certain man and another than between a certain man and a certain beast. It is, therefore, not so much the understanding that constitutes the specific difference between man and the animals as his capacity as a free agent. Nature commands every animal and the beast obeys. Man feels the same impulse, but he knows he is free to acquiesce or to resist; and it is above all in the awareness of this freedom that the spirituality of his soul is displayed, for physics in some way explains the mechanism of the senses and the formation of ideas, but, in the power of willing, or rather of choosing, and in the feeling of this power, we find only purely spiritual acts, which cannot be explained by the laws of mechanics.

But even if the difficulties that surround all these issues should leave some room for raising questions about this difference between man and animal, there is another very specific quality that distinguishes them and about which there can be no dispute: this is the faculty of perfecting oneself, a faculty that, with the aid of circumstances, successively develops all the others and resides in us, as much in the species as in the individual, unlike an animal, which is, at the end of a few months, what it will be all its life, and its species, at the end of a thousand years, what it was the first year of that thousand. Why is man alone prone to becoming an imbecile? Is it not that he thus returns to his original state and that, while the beast, which has acquired nothing and which has nothing more to lose, is always left with its instinct, man, losing once again through old age or other accidents all that his *perfectibility* had made him acquire, thus sinks lower than the beast itself? It would be sad for us to be forced to admit that this distinctive and almost unlimited faculty is the source of all the misfortunes of man; that this faculty, in the course of time, draws him out of that original condition in which he would spend tranquil and innocent days; and that this is what, by causing his knowledge and his errors, his vices and his virtues to emerge over the centuries, makes him, in the long run, a tyrant over himself and over nature.[1] It would be dreadful to be obliged to praise as a beneficent being the one who first suggested to the inhabitant of the banks of the Orinoco the use of those boards he binds to his children's temples and that assure them of at least a part of their imbecility and original happiness.

Left by nature to instinct alone, or rather, compensated for the instincts he may lack with faculties capable first of replacing them and then perhaps of raising him far above nature, savage man will, therefore, begin with purely animal functions: Perceiving and feeling will be his first state, which he will hold in common with all the animals. Willing and not willing, desiring and fearing will be the first and almost the only operations of his soul, until new circumstances cause new developments within it.

Whatever the moralists may say about it, human understanding owes much to the passions, which, it is commonly agreed, also owe much to it. By their activity, our reason is perfected; we seek to know only because we desire enjoyment, and it is impossible to conceive why someone who has neither desires nor fears would take the trouble to reason. The passions, in their turn, draw their origin from our needs and their progress from our knowledge, for we can desire or fear things only on the basis of ideas that we can have about them or through the simple impulse of nature, and savage man, deprived of every sort of enlightenment, experiences only passions of this last kind; his desires do not go past his physical needs.[2] The only goods he knows in the universe are food, a female, and rest; the only evils he fears are pain and hunger; I say pain, and not death, for an animal will never know what it is to die, and knowledge of death and its terrors is one of the first acquisitions that man made in moving away from the animal state.

It would be easy for me, if it were necessary, to support this opinion with facts and to show that, among all the nations of the world, the progress of the mind has been precisely proportionate to the needs the peoples had received from nature or to those to which circumstances had subjected them and, consequently, to the passions that led them to provide for those needs. I would show the arts springing up in Egypt and spreading with the flooding of the Nile; I would follow their progress among the Greeks, where they were seen to germinate, grow, and rise to the heavens among the sands and rocks of Attica without being able to take root on the fertile banks of the Eurotas; I would observe that, in general, the peoples of the North are more industrious than those of the South because they can less afford not to be so, as if nature, in this way, wanted to equalize things by giving their minds the fertility it refuses the earth.

But without appealing to the uncertain testimonies of history, who does not see that everything seems to remove savage man from the temptation and means to cease being what he is? His imagination depicts nothing for him; his heart asks nothing of him. His modest needs are so easily found within his reach, and he is so far from the level of knowledge necessary for wanting to acquire greater knowledge, that he can have neither foresight nor curiosity. The spectacle of nature becomes unimportant to him, by dint of becoming familiar. It is always the same order, it is always the same revolutions; he does not have the mind to be surprised at the greatest marvels, and we must not seek within him the philosophy that man needs in order to know how to observe just once what he has seen every day. His soul, which nothing agitates, is given over to the sentiment of its present existence alone, without any idea of the future, however near it may be, and his plans, as limited as his views, hardly extend to the end of the day. Such is, even today, the Carib's degree of foresight; he sells his cotton bed in the morning and comes weeping in the evening to buy it back, for want of having foreseen that he would need it for the next night.

The more we ponder this subject, the greater the distance from pure sensations to the simplest knowledge grows in our eyes, and it is impossible to conceive how a man, through his own strength alone, without the help of communication, and without the goad of necessity, could have bridged so great a gap. How many centuries may have passed by before men were in a position to see any fire other than that from the heavens? How many different chances did they need to learn the most common uses of this element? How many times did they let it die out before they acquired the art of reproducing it? And how many times may each of these secrets have died with the one who discovered it? What shall we say about agriculture, an art that requires so much labor and foresight, that draws on other arts, that is quite clearly feasible only in a society that is at least in its beginnings, and that serves us not so much to get from the earth foods it would easily provide without cultivation, as to force from it preferences that are more to our taste? But let us suppose that men had multiplied to the point that the natural products would no longer have sufficed to feed them, a supposition which, it may be said in passing, would reveal a great advantage for the human species in this way of living. Let us suppose that without forges and workshops, the tools for plowing had fallen from the heavens into the hands of the savages; that these men had overcome the mortal hatred they all have for continuous labor; that they had learned to fore-see their needs so far in advance; that they had guessed how the earth must be cultivated, grains sown, and trees planted; that they had discovered the art of milling grain and fermenting grapes, all things that must have been taught to them by the gods, since it is impossible to conceive how they could have learned them on their own. After that, who would be the man mad enough to torment himself by cultivating a field that will be stripped bare by the first comer, man or beast alike, for whom this crop is suitable; and how could each man resolve to spend his life at hard labor, the reward from which is all the more necessary to him the more certain he is of not reap-ing it? In a word, how could this situation lead men to cultivate the land as long as it is not divided up among them, that is to say, as long as the state of nature has not been obliterated?

Even if we wish to suppose a savage man as skillful in the art of thinking as our philosophers make him out to be; even if we should, following their example, make a philosopher of him, discovering on his own the most sublime truths, creating for himself, by chains of highly abstract reasoning, maxims of justice and reason derived from the love of order in general or the known will of his creator; in a word, even if we would assume in his mind as much intelligence and enlightenment as it must have and in which we actually find dullness and stupidity, what use would the species make of all this metaphysics, which could not be communicated and which would perish with the individual who had invented it? What progress could the human race make scattered in the woods among the animals? And to what degree could men mutually perfect and enlighten each other, who, having neither a fixed domicile nor any need of one another, would perhaps meet barely twice in their lives, without knowing each other and without speaking to each other?

Let us consider how many ideas we owe to the use of speech, how much grammar trains and facilitates the operations of the mind; and let us think of the incredible efforts and infinite time that the initial invention of languages must have cost; let us join these reflections to the preceding ones, and we shall judge how many thousands of centuries would have been necessary to develop successively in the human mind the operations of which it was capable.

Allow me to consider, for a moment, the obstacles to the origin of languages. I could content myself with citing or repeating here the research that the Abbé de Condillac° has done on this subject, which all fully confirms my opinion, and which perhaps gave me my first idea about it. But since the way in which this philosopher resolves the objections that he himself raises about the origin of instituted signs shows that he has assumed what I bring into question, namely, a kind of society already established among the inventors of language, I believe that in referring to his thoughts on this matter, I should add my own in order to expose the same difficulties to the light of day that are appropriate to my subject. The first one that presents itself is to imagine how languages could become necessary, for since men had no connections with each other, nor any need of them, it is impossible to understand either the necessity for this invention or even its possibility, if it was not indispensable. I would just say, like many others, that languages were born in the domestic intercourse among fathers, mothers, and children, but, aside from the fact that this would not resolve the difficulties, it would be making the mistake of those who, in reasoning about the state of nature, transfer into it ideas acquired in society; they always see the family gathered together in a single dwelling, with its members maintaining among themselves a union as intimate and permanent as that among us, in which so many common interests unite them. Instead, in this primitive state, where, having neither houses nor huts nor property of any kind, each one took shelter at random, and often for only one night; males and females united fortuitously, depending on chance encounters, opportunity, and desire, without speech being a much-needed interpreter of what they had to say to each other; they parted from each other with the same ease. The mother at first nursed her children for her own needs; later, once habit had endeared them to her, she nourished them for their own. As soon as they had the strength to seek their own food, they did not take long to leave the mother herself, and since there was almost no other way of finding each other again except by not losing sight of each other, they were soon at the point of not even recognizing each other. Notice again that since the child has to explain all his needs and, consequently, has more to say to the mother than the mother to the child, it is the child who must make the greatest efforts to invent language, and that the language he uses must be largely of his own making, which would generate as many languages as there are individuals to speak them; the wandering, vagabond life, which gives no idiom time to become consistent, contributes even more to this multiplication, for to say that the mother teaches the child the words he must use to ask her for this thing or that clearly shows how already developed languages are taught, but it does not tell us how they developed.

Let us suppose this initial difficulty has been overcome. Let us, for a moment, cross over the immense distance that must have existed between the pure state of nature and the need for languages; and, assuming them to be necessary, let us seek how they might have begun to establish themselves. A new difficulty arises, worse still than the preceding one, for, if men needed speech to learn how to think, they needed still more to know how to think in order to discover the art of speaking; and even if we understood how vocal sounds were taken as the conventional expressions of our ideas, it would still remain for us to discover what the conventional expressions may have been for ideas that, having no tangible object, could not be indicated either by gesture or by voice. For this reason, we are scarcely able to formulate tenable conjectures about the birth of this art of communicating our thoughts and establishing intercourse between minds, a sublime art that is already quite far from its origin, but which the philosopher still sees at such a prodigious distance from its perfection that there is no man bold enough to affirm that it will ever reach it, even if the revolutions time necessarily brings about were suspended in its favor, and if prejudices were thrown out of the academies or stood silent before them, and even if they were able to occupy themselves with this thorny problem for many centuries without interruption.

Man's first language, the most universal, the most energetic, and the only one he needed before it became necessary to persuade men gathered together, is the cry of nature. Since this cry was wrung from him only by a kind of instinct in pressing circumstances to beg for help in great dangers, or for relief from violent ills, it was not of great use in the ordinary course of life, where more moderate feelings prevail. When the ideas of men began to spread and multiply and closer communication was established among them, they sought more numerous signs and a more extensive language. They multiplied vocal inflections and combined them with gestures, which, by their nature, are more expressive and whose meaning depends less on a prior decision. They therefore expressed visible and mobile objects by means of gestures and audible ones by means of imitative sounds, but since a gesture scarcely indicates anything but objects present or easily described and visible actions; since its use is not universal, because darkness or the interposition of a body renders it useless; and since it requires rather than arouses attention, men finally thought of substituting vocal articulations, which, without having the same relationship to certain ideas, are more likely to represent them all as established signs. Such a substitution could only be made by common consent and in a way rather difficult to put into practice for men whose crude organs had as yet no training, and still more difficult to conceive in itself, since that unanimous agreement had to be motivated in some way, and since speech appears to have been quite necessary in order to establish the use of speech.

It must be assumed that the first words men used had, in their mind, a much broader meaning than do those used in languages already formed, and that, ignoring the division of speech into its constituent parts, they at first gave each word the meaning of an entire sentence. When they began to distinguish subject from predicate, and verb from noun, which was no mediocre effort of genius, substantives were at first only so many proper nouns; the infinitive was the only verb tense; and, with regard to adjectives, any notion of them must have developed only with considerable difficulty, because every adjective is an abstract word, and abstractions are painful and rather unnatural operations of the mind.

At first, each object was given a particular name, without regard to genus and species, which these first founders were not in a position to distinguish, and all individual things presented themselves to their minds in isolation, as they are in the tableau of nature. If one oak tree was called *A*, another was called *B*, so that the more limited their knowledge was, the more extensive their dictionary became. The awkwardness of all this nomenclature could not be easily eliminated, for in order to arrange beings under common and generic denominations, it was necessary to know their properties and differences; observations and definitions were necessary, that is to say, far more natural history and metaphysics than the men of those times could possess.

Moreover, general ideas can be introduced into the mind only with the help of words, and the understanding grasps them only through sentences. This is one of the reasons why animals can neither form such ideas nor ever acquire the perfectibility that depends upon them. When a monkey moves unhesitatingly from one nut to another, does anyone think that he has the general idea of this type of fruit and that he compares its archetype with these two individual nuts? Undoubtedly not, but the sight of one of these nuts recalls to his memory the sensations he received from the other, and his eyes, modified in a certain way, announce to his sense of taste the modification it is about to receive. Every general idea is purely intellectual; if the imagination is involved, the idea immediately becomes particular. Try to draw for yourself the image of a tree in general; you will never succeed in doing it; in spite of yourself, you must see it as small or large, sparse or bushy, light or dark, and if it depends on you to see in it nothing but what is found in every tree, this image would no longer resemble a tree. Purely abstract beings are seen in the same way, or are understood only through discourse. The definition alone of a triangle gives you the true idea of it. As soon as you picture one in your mind, it is a particular triangle and not another, and you cannot avoid making its lines perceptible or its plane colored. It is therefore necessary to utter sentences; it is therefore necessary to speak in order to have general ideas, for as soon as the imagination stops, the mind goes no further without the help of speech. If the first inventors of speech could, therefore, give names only to the ideas they already had, it follows that the first substantives could never have been anything but proper nouns.

But when, by means I cannot conceive, our new grammarians began to extend their ideas and to generalize their words, the ignorance of the inventors must have subjected this method to very strict limits; and just as they had at first excessively multiplied the names of individual things, for lack of knowing the genera and species, they later created too few species and genera for lack of having considered beings in all their differences. In order to push the divisions far enough, it would have required more experience and knowledge than they could have had and more research and labor than they were willing to expend on it. Now if even at present, new species are discovered every day that until now had escaped all our observations, just think how many of them must have been hidden from men who judged things only on first appearances! As for the primitive categories and the most general notions, it is superfluous to add that they, too, must have escaped them. How, for example, would they have imagined or understood the words *matter, mind, substance, mode, figure,* and *movement,* since our philosophers, who have been using them for such a long time, have themselves great difficulty in understanding them, and since the ideas attached to these words are purely metaphysical, they found no model for them in nature?

I must stop at these first steps, and I beg my judges to suspend their reading here to consider, concerning the invention of physical substantives alone, that is, concerning the easiest part of the language to come up with, the distance it still had to go in order to express all the thoughts of men, assume a constant form, be spoken in public, and have an influence upon society. I beg them to think about how much time and knowledge were necessary to discover numbers, abstract words, aorists, and all the tenses of verbs, particles, syntax, the linking of sentences, reasoning, and to develop all the logic of discourse. As for myself, alarmed by difficulties that multiply and convinced of the nearly demonstrable impossibility that languages could have arisen and been established by purely human means, I leave to anyone who wants to undertake it the discussion of this difficult problem: Which was more necessary, a society already bound together for the invention of languages, or already invented languages for the establishment of society?

Whatever these origins may be, at least we see, from the little care nature has taken to bring men closer together through mutual needs and to facilitate their use of speech, how little it has prepared them for sociability, and how little it has contributed of its own to all they have done to establish social bonds. Indeed, it is impossible to imagine why, in that primitive state, one man would sooner need another man than a monkey or a wolf its fellow creature, or, assuming this need, what motive could commit the other to provide for it, or even, in the latter case, how they could agree among themselves on the conditions. I know that we are told again and again that nothing could have been so miserable as man in the state of nature, and if it is true, as I believe I have proved, that only after many centuries could he have had the desire and the opportunity to leave that state, this would be a complaint to lodge against nature and not against the one whom nature had thus constituted. But, if I correctly understand this term *miserable*, it is a word that makes no sense or that signifies only a painful privation and the suffering of body or soul. Now, I would very much like someone to explain to me what kind of misery there can be for a free being, whose heart is at peace and whose body is healthy. I ask which of them, civil or natural life, is more prone to becoming unbearable for those who enjoy it. We see around us almost no one but people who complain about their existence, even some who deprive themselves of it insofar as it is in their power, and the combination of divine and human laws scarcely suffices to put a stop to this disorder. I ask if anyone has ever heard it said that a savage living free has even dreamed of complaining about life and of killing himself. Let us therefore judge, with less pride, the side on which true misery lies. Nothing, on the contrary, would have been so miserable as savage man dazzled by knowledge, tormented by passions, and reasoning about a state different from his own. It was through a very wise providence that the potential faculties he possessed were to develop only with the opportunities to exercise them, so that they might be neither superfluous and burdensome to him ahead of time, nor overdue and useless when needed. He had in instinct alone all that he needed to live in the state of nature; he has in cultivated reason only what he needs to live in society.

It appears at first that men in that state, having among themselves no kind of moral relationship nor any known duties, could be neither good nor evil and had neither vices nor virtues, unless, taking these words in a physical sense, we call vices the qualities in the individual that can harm his own preservation and virtues those which can contribute to it, in which case, it would be necessary to call the most virtuous the one who least resists the simple impulses of nature. But without departing from the ordinary sense of the words, it is appropriate to suspend the judgment we might bring to such a situation and to distrust our prejudices, until, with scales in hand, we have examined whether there are more virtues than vices among civilized men; or whether their virtues are more advantageous than their vices are disastrous; or whether the progress of their knowledge is sufficient compensation for the wrongs they do to each other as they learn of the good they ought to do for each other; or whether they would not be, all things considered, in a happier situation, having neither harm to fear nor good to hope for from anyone, rather than subjecting themselves to universal dependence and obligating themselves to receive everything from those who are not obligated to give them anything.

Above all, let us not conclude with Hobbes that for want of any idea of goodness, man is naturally evil; that he is vicious because he does not know virtue; that he always refuses his fellow creatures any services he does not believe he owes them; or that, by virtue of the right he claims with reason to the things he needs, he foolishly imagines himself to be the sole owner of the entire universe. Hobbes has very clearly seen the flaw in all modern definitions of natural right, but the conclusions he draws from his own demonstrate that he takes it in a sense that is no less false. Reasoning upon the principles he establishes, this author should have said that the state of nature, being the one in which our concern for self-preservation is least prejudicial to that of others, was, consequently, the state best suited to peace and the most fitting for the human race. He says precisely the opposite, as a result of having inappropriately brought into savage man's concern for self-preservation the need to satisfy a multitude of passions that are the handiwork of society, and that have made laws necessary. The evil man, he says, is a robust child; it remains to be seen whether savage man is a robust child. Even if we were to grant this to him, what would we conclude from it? That if this man were as dependent on others when he is robust as when he is weak, there is no sort of excess to which he would not be inclined; that he would beat his mother when she was too slow in giving him her breast; that he would strangle one of his younger brothers when he was bothered by him; that he would bite another's leg when he was struck or disturbed by it. But being robust and being dependent are two contradictory suppositions in the state of nature; man is weak when he is dependent, and he is emancipated before he is robust. Hobbes did not see that the same cause that prevents savages from using their reason, as our jurists claim they do, prevents them, at the same time, from abusing their faculties, as Hobbes himself claims they do, so that it could be said that savages are not wicked precisely because they do not know what it is to be good, for it is neither the development of knowledge nor the restraint of law, but the calmness of the passions and ignorance of vice which prevent them from doing evil: *tanto plus in illis proficit vitiorum ignoratio, quam in his cognitio virtutis.*° There is, moreover, another principle that Hobbes did not perceive and which, having been given to man to moderate, under certain circumstances, the ferocity of his self-love, or before the birth of this love, the desire for self-preservation,[3] tempers the ardor he has for his own well-being through an innate repugnance to seeing his fellow man suffer. I do not believe I have any contradiction to fear in granting to man the only natural virtue that the most excessive detractor of human virtues has been forced to recognize. I am speaking of compassion, a disposition fitting for beings as weak and as subject to as many ills as we are, a virtue all the more universal and all the more useful to man, since it precedes within him any use of reflection, and so natural that the beasts themselves sometimes show perceptible signs of it. Without speaking of the tenderness of mothers for their young and of the perils they brave to protect them, we observe everyday the repugnance horses have to trampling a living body. An animal does not, without uneasiness, pass close by a dead member of its species; there are even some that give them a kind of burial; and the sad lowing of cattle entering a slaughterhouse bespeaks the impression they receive from the horrible spectacle that strikes them. We see with pleasure the author of the *Fable of the Bees*, forced to recognize man as a compassionate and sensitive being, to depart from his cold and subtle style, in the example he gives, in order to offer us the pathetic image of a confined man who beholds a ferocious beast outside ripping a child from his mother's breast, crushing his weak limbs with its murderous teeth, and tearing apart with its claws the palpitating entrails of this child. What dreadful agitation will he not feel, this witness of an event in which he takes no personal interest? What anguish will he not suffer at this sight, being unable to provide help to the fainting mother and the dying child?

Such is the pure movement of nature, prior to all reflection; such is the force of natural compassion, which the most depraved moral habits still have difficulty destroying, since we see everyday in our theaters, moved and weeping over the misfortunes of an unfortunate, the kind of man who, if he were in the tyrant's place, would increase his enemy's torments even more. Mandeville strongly felt that with all their morals, men would never have been anything but monsters, if nature had not given them compassion in support of reason, but he did not see that from this quality alone arise all the social virtues he wants to dispute in men. Indeed, what are generosity, clemency, humanity, if not compassion applied to the weak, to the guilty, or to the human species in general? Benevolence and even friendship are, strictly speaking, the products of constant compassion fixed upon a particular object, for is to desire that someone not suffer anything other than to desire that he be happy? Even if it were true that commiseration is only a feeling that puts us in the place of the one who is suffering, a feeling that is vague and strong in savage man, developed but weak in civilized man, what importance would this idea have concerning the truth of what I say other than to give it greater force? Indeed, commiseration will be all the more energetic the more intimately the onlooking animal identifies with the suffering animal. Now, it is evident that this identification must have been infinitely closer in the state of nature than in the state of reasoning. It is reason that engenders self-love,° and it is reflection that strengthens it; it is reason that makes man look inward; it separates him from all that disturbs and distresses him. It is philosophy that isolates him; it is through philosophy that he says in secret, at the sight of a suffering man: "Perish if you will, I am safe." No longer can anything but dangers to the entire society trouble the tranquil sleep of the philosopher and tear him from his bed. His fellow man may have his throat slit with impunity under his window; the philosopher has only to put his hands over his ears and argue with himself a little to prevent nature, which rebels within him, from making him identify with the one who is being murdered. Savage man does not have this admirable talent; and for want of wisdom and reason, he is always seen surrendering without a thought to the first sentiment of humanity. In riots, in street fights, the populace gathers and the prudent man withdraws; it is the rabble, the women of the marketplace, who separate the combatants and who prevent decent people from slitting each other's throats.

It is, therefore, very certain that compassion is a natural sentiment, which, by moderating in each individual the activity of love of self,° helps bring about the mutual preservation of the whole species. It is compassion that carries us without reflection to the aid of those we see suffering; it is compassion in the state of nature that takes the place of laws, moral habits, and virtue, with the advantage that no one is tempted to disobey its gentle voice; it will deter any robust savage from robbing a weak child or an infirm old man of his subsistence acquired with difficulty, if he himself hopes to be able to find his own elsewhere. Instead of that sublime maxim of reasoned justice, *Do unto others as you would have them do unto you*, it inspires in all men that other maxim of natural goodness, much less perfect but perhaps more useful than the preceding one: *Do what is good for you with the least possible harm to others*. It is, in a word, in this natural sentiment rather than in subtle arguments that we must seek the cause of the repugnance every man would feel at doing evil, even independently of the maxims of education. Although it may be possible for Socrates and minds of that caliber to acquire virtue through reason, the human race would have ceased to exist long ago, if its preservation had only depended upon the reasonings of those who belong to it.

With such inactive passions and such salutary restraint, men, wild rather than evil and more mindful of protecting themselves from the harm they might experience than tempted to do any to others, were not subject to very dangerous quarrels. Since they had no kind of dealings with each other; since they knew, consequently, neither vanity nor respect, nor esteem nor contempt; since they had not the least notion of yours and mine, nor any real idea of justice; since they regarded the violence they might endure as a wrong easily redressed and not as an injury that must be punished; and since they did not even dream of vengeance, unless it was perhaps without thinking and on the spot, like the dog who bites the stone that is thrown at him, their disputes would rarely have had bloody consequences if they had not had a subject more sensitive than food. But I see a more dangerous one that remains for me to discuss.

Among the passions that stir the heart of man, there is an ardent, impetuous one that makes one sex necessary to the other, a terrible passion that braves all dangers, over-comes all obstacles, and that, in its fury, seems capable of destroying the human race it is destined to preserve. What will men become, prey to this unbridled and brutal rage, without modesty, without restraint, and fighting every day over the objects of their love affairs at the price of their blood?

It must first of all be admitted that the more violent the passions, the more necessary laws are to contain them, but, besides the fact that the disorders and crimes they cause among us daily show well enough the insufficiency of the laws in this regard, it would still be good to examine whether these disorders were not born with the laws themselves, for then, even if the laws were capable of quell-ing them, the very least we should require of them is that they put a stop to an evil that would not exist without them.

Let us begin by distinguishing the moral from the physical in the sentiment of love. The physical is that gen-eral desire that brings one sex to unite with the other; the moral is what defines this desire and fixes it exclusively upon a single object, or at least gives it a greater degree of energy for this preferred object. Now, it is easy to see that the moral aspect of love is an artificial sentiment, born of social custom and celebrated by women with great skill and care to establish their influence and to make domi-nant the sex that should obey. This sentiment, being founded on certain notions of merit or beauty a savage is not in a position to have, and on comparisons he is not in a position to make, must mean almost nothing to him, for, as his mind could not form abstract ideas of regularity and proportion, his heart is not susceptible to the sentiments of admiration and love, which, even without being perceived, arise from the application of these ideas; he listens solely to the temperament he has received from nature and not to the taste he has been unable to acquire, and any woman is good for him.

Limited solely to the physical aspect of love, and for-
tunate enough to be unaware of those preferences that
inflame this sentiment and increase the difficulties it
causes, men must feel the ardors of their temperament less
frequently and less sharply, and, consequently, have fewer
and less cruel disputes among themselves. Imagination,
which wreaks so much havoc among us, does not speak
to savage hearts; each peacefully awaits the impulse of
nature, gives himself over to it without choice, with more
pleasure than fury, and, once the need is satisfied, all
desire is extinguished.

It is, therefore, incontestable that love itself, like all the
other passions, has acquired only in society that impetuous ardor that so often makes it fatal to men, and it is all
the more ridiculous to portray savages as constantly
slaughtering each other to satisfy their brutality, since this
opinion is directly contrary to experience, and since the
Caribs, who, among all existing peoples have, until now,
deviated least from the state of nature, are precisely the
most peaceful in their love affairs and the least subject to
jealousy, even though they live in a scorching climate,
which always seems to cause these passions to grow more
active.

With regard to the inferences that might be drawn
about several species of animals from fights between the
males that always bloody our farmyards or that make our
forests resound with their cries in the springtime as they
fight over the female, it is necessary to begin by excluding
all species in which nature has obviously established in the
comparative strength of the sexes relations other than
those among us. Thus, cockfights have no implications for
the human species. In species where proportion is better
observed, these fights can only be caused by the scarcity
of females in relation to the number of males, or the
specific intervals during which the female always refuses
the advances of the male, which amounts to the same

thing, for if each female only tolerates the male during two months of the year, it is, in this regard, as if the number of females were reduced by five sixths. Now, neither of these two cases is applicable to the human species, in which the number of females generally surpasses that of males and in which, even among the savages, females have never been observed to have periods of heat and exclusion, like those of other species. Moreover, since among several of these animals the entire species comes into heat at the same time, there comes a terrible moment of common ardor, tumult, disorder, and fighting, a moment that does not come about in the human species, in which love is never periodic. We cannot, therefore, conclude from the fighting of certain animals for the possession of females that the same thing would happen to man in the state of nature, and even if we could draw this conclusion, as these conflicts do not destroy the other species, we should at least think that they would not be more deadly to ours. And it is quite apparent that they would raise less havoc in the state of nature than in society, especially in the countries where, since moral habits still count for some-thing, the jealousy of lovers and the vengeance of husbands every day cause duels, murders, and even worse; where the duty of eternal fidelity serves only to create adulterers; and where the laws of continence and honor themselves necessarily spread debauchery and multiply abortions.

Let us conclude that, wandering in the forests, with-out industry, without speech, without homes, without war, and without ties, with no need of his fellow human beings, nor any desire to harm them, perhaps without ever even recognizing any of them individually, savage man, subject to few passions and self-sufficient, had only the sentiments and knowledge appropriate to that state; that he felt only his true needs and looked only at what he believed he had an interest in seeing; and that his intel-ligence made no more progress than his vanity. If by chance he made some discovery, he was all the less able to communicate it, because he did not even recognize his own children. Art perished with the inventor; there was neither education nor progress; the generations multiplied in vain; and since each one always started from the same point, centuries passed by in all the crudeness of the earliest ages; the species was already old, and man remained ever a child.

If I have dwelled so long upon the assumption of this primitive condition, it is because, having ancient errors and inveterate prejudices to destroy, I thought I must dig down to the roots and show in the picture of the true state of nature how far even natural inequality is from having as much reality and influence in this state as our writers claim.

Indeed, it is easy to see that among the differences that distinguish men, several pass for natural that are exclusively the work of habit and the various types of life that men adopt in society. Thus, a robust or delicate temperament, the strength or weakness that depends upon it, often come more from the harsh or effeminate manner in which one has been raised than from the original constitution of the body. It is the same with strength of mind, and not only does education produce a difference between cultivated minds and those that are not, but it increases the one that exists among the former in proportion to their knowledge, for if a giant and a dwarf walk on the same road, each step they take will give a new advantage to the giant. Now if we compare the prodigious diversity of the kinds of education and types of life that prevail in different orders of the civil state with the simplicity and uniformity of animal and savage life, where all nourish themselves on the same foods, live in the same manner, and do exactly the same things, we will understand how much less the difference from man to man must be in the state of nature than in that of society, and how much natural inequality must increase in the human species through the inequality of social institutions.

But even if nature were to assign as many preferences in the distribution of its gifts as is claimed, what advantage would the most favored get from them to the detriment of others, in a state of things that would admit of almost no kind of relationship among them? Where there is no love, of what use is beauty? What will wit mean to people who do not speak, and cunning to those who have no dealings with others? I always hear it repeated that the strongest will oppress the weak, but let someone explain to me what is meant by this word *oppression*. Some will dominate by violence, others will moan, enslaved by all their whims. That is precisely what I observe among us, but I do not see how it could be said of savage men, to whom it would be very difficult even to explain what servitude and domination are. One man might well seize the fruits another has gathered, the game he has killed, the cave that served him as shelter, but how will he ever succeed in making himself obeyed, and what chains of dependence could there be among men who possess nothing? If someone chases me from one tree, I am free to go to another; if someone torments me in one place, who will prevent me from going elsewhere? Is there a man with strength sufficiently superior to mine, and, in addition, sufficiently depraved, sufficiently lazy, and sufficiently ferocious to force me to provide for his subsistence while he remains idle? He must resolve not to lose sight of me for a single instant, to keep me very carefully tied down while he is asleep, for fear I may escape or kill him; that is to say, he is obliged to expose himself voluntarily to a difficulty much greater than the one he wants to avoid and the one he causes for me. After all this, what if he momentarily relaxes his vigilance? What if an unforeseen noise makes him turn his head? I take twenty steps into the forest, my chains are broken, and he never in his life sees me again.

Without uselessly prolonging these details, I must make everyone see that since the bonds of servitude are formed merely from the mutual dependence of men and from the reciprocal needs that unite them, it is impossible to enslave a man without first having put him in the position of being unable to do without another: Since this situation did not exist in the state of nature, it leaves everyone free of the yoke and makes the law of the strongest meaningless.

After having proven that inequality is scarcely perceptible in the state of nature, and that its influence there is almost nonexistent, it remains for me to show its origin and progress in the successive developments of the human mind. After having shown that *perfectibility*, the social virtues, and the other faculties that natural man had received potentially could never develop by themselves, that to do so they needed the accidental combination of several unrelated causes which might never have arisen, and without which man would have remained eternally in his primitive condition, it remains for me to consider and to compare the different accidents that were able to develop human reason while damaging the species, make a being wicked while making him sociable, and, from so distant a beginning, finally, bring man and the world to the point where we now see them.

I admit that since the events I have to describe could have happened in various ways, I can make my choices only through conjectures, but, besides the fact that these conjectures become reasons, when they are the most probable that can be drawn from the nature of things and the sole means of discovering the truth, the consequences that I want to deduce from mine will not for that reason be conjectural, since, on the basis of the principles I have just established, no other system could be formulated which would not furnish me with the same results and from which I could not draw the same conclusions.

This will excuse me from extending my reflections on the manner in which the lapse of time compensates for the improbability of the events; on the surprising power of very minor causes, even when they are in constant operation; on the impossibility, on the one hand, of destroying certain hypotheses, though, on the other, they cannot be given the same degree of certainty as facts; on how two facts, given as real, are linked by a series of intermediary facts that are unknown or regarded as such, and how it is within the province of history, when it exists, to supply the facts that link them, or within the province of philosophy, in the absence of history, to determine similar facts that would link them; and finally, on how the similarity of events reduces the facts to a much smaller number of different classes than might be imagined. It suffices for me to offer these matters for the consideration of my judges; it suffices for me to have arranged things so that the common reader would have no need to consider them.

## Part 2

The first one who, having fenced off a plot of land, dared to say "This is mine" and found people simple enough to believe him was the real founder of civil society. What crimes, wars, murders, what miseries and horrors would the human race have been spared had the one who, upon pulling up the stakes or filling in the ditch, shouted to his fellow men, "Beware of listening to this imposter; you are lost, if you forget that the fruits of the earth belong to all and that the earth belongs to no one." But it is quite apparent that by that time, things had already come to the point where they could no longer go on as they were, for this idea of property, depending upon many prior ideas that could only have arisen successively, did not suddenly form in the human mind. It was necessary to make much progress, to acquire considerable skill and knowledge, and to transmit and increase them from age to age, before arriving at this last stage of the state of nature. Let us, therefore, go further back into these matters, and let us endeavor to gather together under a single point of view that slow succession of events and experiences in their most natural order.

Man's first sentiment was that of his own existence, his first concern was that for his own preservation. The products of the earth furnished him with all the help he needed; instinct led him to make use of them. Since hunger and other appetites made him experience, by turns, various ways of existing, there was one of them that invited him to perpetuate his species; and this blind inclination, devoid of any sentiment of the heart, only produced a purely animal act. Once the need was satisfied, the two sexes no longer recognized each other, and even the child no longer meant anything to the mother, as soon as he could do without her.

Such was the condition of man at his beginnings; such was the life of an animal limited at first to pure sensations, barely profiting from the gifts that nature offered him, far from dreaming of wresting anything from it. But difficulties soon arose; it was necessary to learn to surmount them—the height of trees, which prevented him from reaching their fruits, the competition of animals, who were seeking to feed on them, or the ferocity of those who sought his life; everything obliged him to apply himself to bodily exercise; it was necessary to make himself agile, swift of foot, vigorous in combat. Natural arms, such as the branches of trees and stones, were soon discovered at hand. He learned to surmount nature's obstacles, to combat other animals if necessary, to fight for his subsistence even with other men, or to make up for what he had to yield to the stronger.

As the human race spread, difficulties multiplied along with men. Differences in land, climates, and seasons could force them to make changes in their ways of living. Barren years, long and hard winters, scorching summers that consume everything demanded new skills from them. Along the seashores and the riverbanks they invented the line and hook and became fishermen and fish eaters. In the forests, they made bows and arrows and became hunters and warriors; in cold countries, they wrapped themselves in the skins of beasts they had slain; lightning, a volcano, or some happy accident acquainted them with fire, a new resource against the harshness of winter. They learned to preserve this element, then to reproduce it, and, finally, to use it to prepare meats they had previously devoured raw.

This repeated use of beings different from himself and from each other must naturally have engendered in man's mind perceptions of certain relations. Those relationships that we express with the words large, small, strong, weak, fast, slow, fearful, bold, and other similar ideas, compared when necessary and almost without thinking about it, finally produced in him some kind of reflection, or rather, an automatic prudence that indicated to him the precautions most necessary for his safety.

The new knowledge that resulted from this development increased his superiority over the other animals by making him aware of it. He practiced setting traps for them; he misled them in a thousand ways; and, although several surpassed him in strength at combat or in running speed, he became, in time, the master of those that could serve him and the scourge of those that could harm him. In this way, the first glance he cast upon himself produced in him the first impulse of pride; in this way, still hardly knowing how to make distinctions of rank and considering himself in the first rank by virtue of his species, he prepared himself from afar to lay claim to first rank as an individual.

Although his fellow men were not for him what they are for us, and although he had scarcely more dealings with them than with other animals, they were not forgotten in his observations. The correspondences that time could make him perceive among them, his female and himself, made him assess those he did not perceive, and, seeing that all behaved as he himself would have done under similar circumstances, he concluded that their way of thinking and feeling was entirely in keeping with his own, and this important truth, firmly established in his mind, made him follow, by a presentiment as sure as dialectic and more quick, the best rules of conduct it was suitable for him to observe toward them for his own advantage and safety.

Taught by experience that love of well-being is the sole motive of human actions, he found himself in a position to distinguish the rare occasions when common interest could make him rely on the assistance of his fellow men, and those still rarer occasions when competition could make him challenge them. In the first case, he united with them in a herd or at the very most in some sort of free association that obligated no one and that lasted only as long as the passing need that had created it. In the second, each sought his own advantage, either by open force, if he believed he could, or by cleverness and cunning, if he felt himself the weakest.

In that way, men were able imperceptibly to acquire some crude idea of mutual commitments and of the advantage of fulfilling them, but only as far as present and palpable interest could demand, for foresight meant nothing to them, and far from dealing with a distant future, they hardly thought of the next day. If it was a matter of catching a deer, each certainly felt that for this purpose he ought to remain faithfully at his post, but if a hare happened to pass within reach of one of them, it must not be doubted that he pursued it without any scruples and that, having seized his prey, he cared very little about causing his companions to miss theirs.

It is easy to understand that such dealings did not require a language much more refined than that of crows or monkeys, which gather together in nearly the same way. Inarticulate cries, many gestures, and some imitative noises must have composed the universal language for a long time; by adding to these in each region a few articulated and conventional sounds, the institution of which, as I have already said, is not very easily explained, particular languages arose, but crude, imperfect ones, somewhat like those of various savage nations today. I am traveling across many centuries like a shaft of light, forced on by the passing of time, by the abundance of things I have to say, and by the almost imperceptible progress of the beginnings, for the more slowly events followed one another, the more swiftly they can be described.

These first advances finally put men within reach of making more rapid ones. The more the mind became enlightened, the more skills developed. Soon, ceasing to fall asleep under the first tree or to retreat into caves, they discovered some kinds of axes made of hard, sharp stones, which served for cutting wood, digging the earth, and making huts from branches, which they later thought of coating with clay and mud. This was the epoch of a first revolution, which brought about the establishment of the family and the distinction between families, and which introduced a sort of property, from which perhaps already many quarrels and fights arose. Yet, since the strongest were probably the first to build themselves lodgings they felt capable of defending, the weak presumably found it quicker and safer to imitate them than to attempt to dislodge them, and, as for those who already had huts, each must rarely have sought to appropriate that of his neighbor, less because it did not belong to him than because it was useless to him, and because he could not seize it without exposing himself to a very fierce fight with the family who was occupying it.

The first developments of the heart were the effect of a new situation that brought together husbands and wives, fathers and children in a common dwelling; the habit of living together gave rise to the sweetest sentiments known to men: conjugal love and paternal love. Each family became a small society all the better united because mutual attachment and liberty were its only bonds, and it was then that the first difference was established in the manner of living of the two sexes, who, until then, had had but one. Women became more sedentary and grew accustomed to tending the hut and the children, while the men went out to seek their common subsistence. Through living a slightly softer life, the two sexes also began to lose something of their ferocity and vigor, but if each one separately became less fit for combatting wild animals, it was easier, on the other hand, to assemble in order to resist them together.

In this new state, with a simple and solitary life, very limited needs, and the tools they had invented to provide for them, men, enjoying a great deal of leisure, used it to obtain various kinds of conveniences unknown to their forefathers; and this was the first yoke they imposed upon themselves without thinking about it and the first source of ills they prepared for their descendants; for besides the fact they continued in this way to grow weak in body and mind, once these conveniences lost almost all their charm through habit and degenerated into true needs, being deprived of them became much more harsh than possessing them was sweet; and people were unhappy to lose them without being happy to possess them.

Here we catch a slightly better glimpse of how the use of speech was established or developed imperceptibly in the bosom of each family, and we may speculate further on how various particular causes could have made language spread and accelerated its progress by making it more necessary. Great floods or earthquakes surrounded inhabited districts with water or ravines; upheavals of the globe detached and broke up portions of the continent into islands. It is conceivable that among men brought together and forced to live together in this way, a common idiom must have formed sooner than among those who roamed freely in the forests of the mainland. Thus it is very possible that after their first attempts at navigation, some islanders brought the use of speech among us, and it is at least highly likely that society and languages originated on islands and were developed there before being known on the mainland.

Everything begins to take on a new appearance. Roaming the woods up to this time, men, having taken to a more settled way of life, slowly come together, unite in various bands, and, finally, in each region, form a particular nation, united by moral habits and characteristics, not by regulations and laws but by the same kind of life and food and by the common influence of climate. In the end, permanent proximity cannot fail to engender some connection between different families. Young people of different sexes live in neighboring huts, the short-lived intercourse required by nature soon leads to another kind, made no less sweet and more permanent by regular contact. People become accustomed to considering different objects and to making comparisons; they acquire imperceptibly ideas of merit and beauty that produce feelings of preference. By virtue of seeing each other, they can no longer do without seeing each other again. A sweet and tender sentiment creeps into their souls and, at the least opposition, becomes an impetuous fury. Jealousy awakens with love, discord triumphs, and the sweetest of the passions receives sacrifices of human blood.

As ideas and feelings succeed one another, as the mind and heart are trained, the human race continues to become tamed, contacts expand, and bonds are tightened. People grew accustomed to assembling in front of their huts or around a large tree: Song and dance, true children of love and leisure, became the amusement, or rather the occupation, of idle men and women gathered together. Each one began to look at the others and to want to be looked at in return, and public esteem came to have a value. The one who sang or danced the best, the most handsome, the strongest, the most skillful, or the most eloquent became the most highly regarded, and this was the first step toward inequality and, at the same time, toward vice.° From these first preferences were born vanity and contempt on the one hand, and shame and envy on the other; and the fermentation caused by these new leavens finally produced compounds fatal to happiness and innocence.

As soon as men had begun to appraise each other and the idea of esteem was formed in their minds, each claimed a right to it, and it was no longer possible to deny it to anyone with impunity. From that arose the first duties of civility, even among savages, and from that every deliberate wrong became an insult, because along with the harm that resulted from the injury, the offended party saw in it a contempt for his person that was often more unbearable than the harm itself. Thus, as each person punished the contempt shown him by others in proportion to his sense of self-worth, acts of vengeance became terrible, and men bloodthirsty and cruel. This is precisely the stage most of the savage peoples known to us have reached; and it is for want of having drawn sufficient distinctions between ideas and of having observed how far these peoples already were from that original state of nature that some have hastened to conclude that man is naturally cruel and that he needs policing to make him gentler, although nothing is so gentle as man in his primitive state, when, placed by nature at an equal distance from the stupidity of beasts and the fatal enlightenment of civil man, and limited equally by instinct and reason to protecting himself from the harm that threatens him, he is restrained by natural compassion from harming anyone himself, without anything leading him to do so, even after he himself has been harmed. For, according to the axiom of the wise Locke, *there can be no injury, where there is no property.*°

But it must be noted that the society already begun and relations among men already established required in them qualities different than those they derived from their primitive constitution; that since morality was beginning to be introduced into human actions, and each man, prior to the existence of laws, was the sole judge and avenger of the injuries he had received, the goodness suitable to the pure state of nature was no longer what was suitable to nascent society; that punishments had to become more severe as the opportunities to offend became more frequent; and that the fear of revenge replaced the restraints of the laws. Thus, although men had become less hardy, and natural compassion had already undergone some deterioration, this period of the development of human faculties, maintaining a happy medium between the indolence of the primitive state and the petulant activity of our self-love,° must have been the happiest and most enduring epoch. The more we reflect upon it, the more we find that this state was the least subject to turmoil, the best for man, and that he must have left it only by some fatal accident that, for the common good, should never have happened. The example of savages, almost all of whom have been found at this stage, seems to confirm that the human race was made to remain there always; that this state is the true youth of the world; and that all the subsequent advances have seemingly been so many steps toward the perfection of the individual, and, in fact, toward the degeneration of the species.

As long as men remained content with their rustic huts, as long as they limited themselves to sewing their clothing made of skins with thorns or fish bones, to adorning themselves with feathers and shells, to painting their bodies with various colors, to improving or embellishing their bows and arrows, to carving a few fishing boats or a few crude musical instruments with sharp stones, in a word, as long as they applied themselves only to tasks that a single man could accomplish and to arts that did not need the cooperation of several hands, they lived free, healthy, good, and happy lives, insofar as they could, given their nature, and continued to enjoy among themselves the sweetness of independent intercourse. But from the moment one man needed help from another, and as soon as they perceived that it was useful for one man to have provisions for two, equality disappeared, property was introduced, work became necessary, and vast forests were turned into pleasant fields that had to be watered with human sweat and in which slavery and misery were soon seen to germinate and grow with the crops.

Metallurgy and agriculture were the two arts whose invention produced this great revolution. For the poet, it is gold and silver, but for the philosopher, it is iron and wheat that civilized men and ruined the human race; both were, consequently, unknown to the savages of America, who for that reason have always remained as they were; other peoples even seem to have remained barbarians as long as they practiced one of these arts without the other; and perhaps one of the best reasons why Europe has been, if not sooner, at least more constantly and more highly civilized than the other parts of the world is that it is both the most abundant in iron and the most fertile for wheat.

It is very difficult to guess how men came to know and to use iron, for it is impossible to believe that, by themselves, they thought of drawing the raw material from the mine and giving it the preparations necessary for melting it down before knowing what the results would be. From another point of view, it is even less possible to attribute this discovery to some accidental fire, because mines form only in arid places, stripped of both trees and plants, so that it appears that nature had taken precautions to conceal this fatal secret from us. There remains, therefore, only the extraordinary circumstance of some volcano that, by belching forth molten metallic materials, gave observers the idea of imitating this operation of nature. Still, it is necessary to assume in them great courage and foresight for undertaking such a difficult task and for envisaging, from afar, the advantages they could derive from it, which scarcely seems possible, except in minds already better trained than theirs must have been.

As for agriculture, its principle was known long before the practice was established, and it is scarcely possible that men, constantly occupied with obtaining their subsistence from trees and plants, would not quickly gain an idea of the means nature uses to grow plants; but their skills only turned in that direction very late, either because trees, which, along with hunting and fishing, supplied their food, did not need their care, or for want of knowing how to use wheat, or for want of tools for cultivating it, or for want of foresight concerning future needs, or, finally, for want of the means to prevent others from appropriating the fruit of their labor. Once they had become more industrious, it is possible to believe that with sharp stones and pointed sticks, they began by cultivating a few vegetables or roots around their huts, long before knowing how to prepare wheat and having the tools necessary for cultivation on a large scale, not to mention that in order to devote oneself to this occupation and to sow the land, one must resolve to lose something at first in order to gain a great deal thereafter, a precaution very far removed from savage man's turn of mind, for, as I have said, he finds it very difficult, in the morning, to think of his needs for the evening.

The invention of the other arts was, therefore, necessary to force the human race to apply itself to that of agriculture. As soon as men were needed to smelt and forge iron, other men were needed to feed them. The more the number of workers came to increase, the fewer hands were employed in supplying the common subsistence, without there being fewer mouths to consume it, and since some needed foodstuffs in exchange for their iron, the others finally discovered the secret of using iron to increase the supply of foodstuffs. From that arose tilling and agriculture, on the one hand, and, on the other, the art of working metals and multiplying their uses.

From the cultivation of lands necessarily followed their division, and from property, once recognized, the first rules of justice, for, in order to render to each his own, each must be able to have something. Moreover, as men began to turn their eyes toward the future, and as all saw themselves with some possessions to lose, there was not one of them who did not have to fear reprisals against himself for the wrongs he might do to others. This origin is all the more natural as it is impossible to conceive of the idea of property arising from anything but manual labor, for it is not apparent what else a man can put into them, besides his own labor, to appropriate things that he has not made. Labor alone, by giving the farmer the right to the produce of the ground he has tilled, consequently, gives him the right to the ground, at least until the harvest, and thus from year to year, what constitutes continuous possession is easily transformed into property. When the ancients, says Grotius, gave Ceres the epithet of legislatrix and the name of Thesmaphoria to a festival celebrated in her honor, they made it understood in this way that the division of lands produced a new kind of right, that is, the right of property, different from the one that results from natural law.

Things in this state could have remained equal, if talents had been equal, and if, for example, the use of iron and the consumption of foodstuffs had always been in exact balance, but this balance that nothing maintained was soon broken; the strongest did more work; the most skillful turned his to better advantage; the most ingenious found ways to curtail his work; the farmer needed more iron, or the blacksmith more wheat; and, by working equally, one earned a great deal, while the other barely had enough to live. Thus, natural inequality spreads imperceptibly along with contrived inequality, and the differences among men, developed by differences in circumstances, make themselves more noticeable, more permanent in their effects, and begin, in the same proportion, to influence the fate of individuals.

Things having reached this point, it is easy to imagine the rest. I shall not stop to describe the successive invention of the other arts, the progress of languages, the testing and use of talents, the inequality of fortunes, the use or abuse of wealth, nor all the details that follow these and that everyone can easily supply. I shall limit myself only to taking a look at the human species placed in this new order of things.

So here, then, are all our faculties developed, memory and imagination in play, self-love° taking an interest, reason made active, and the mind having almost reached the limit of the perfection to which it is susceptible. Behold all the natural qualities put into action, the rank and fate of each man established, not only upon the amount of his property and his power to serve or to harm, but also upon mind, beauty, or skill, upon merit or talents, and since these qualities were the only ones that could attract esteem, it soon became necessary to have them or to feign them; it was necessarily to one's advantage to show oneself to be something other than what one was in fact. To be and to appear became two completely different things, and from this distinction sprang imposing ostentation, deceptive cunning, and all the vices that follow in their train. At the same time, as free and independent as he formerly was, here is man, subjugated, so to speak, by a multitude of new needs to all of nature, and especially to his fellow men, whose slave he becomes, in a sense, even in becoming their master; rich, he needs their services; poor, he needs their help; and even average wealth does not put him in a position to do without them. He must, therefore, constantly seek to interest them in his fate, and to make them find it profitable, either actually or apparently, to work for it. This makes him deceitful and crafty with some, imperious and harsh with others, and makes it necessary for him to abuse all those he needs, when he cannot make them fear him, and when he does not find it in his interest to serve them in a useful way. Finally, consuming ambition, the zeal to elevate his fortune relative to theirs, less out of true need than to set himself above others, inspires in all men a dark inclination to harm each other, a secret jealousy, all the more dangerous because, in order to strike its blow in greater safety, it often assumes the mask of benevolence; in a word, competition and rivalry on the one hand, conflict of interest on the other, and always the hidden desire to profit at the expense of others. All these evils are the first effect of property and the inseparable ramifications of rising inequality.

Before signs to represent wealth had been invented, it could scarcely have consisted of anything but land and livestock, the only real property men can possess. Now, when inheritances had increased in number and size to the point of covering the entire earth and all adjoining one another, some could no longer be enlarged except at the expense of others, and the supernumeraries, whom weakness or laziness had prevented from acquiring anything in their turn, became poor without having lost anything, because, with everything changing around them, they alone had not changed and were obliged to receive or steal their subsistence from the hand of the rich, and from that point domination and servitude, or violence and pillage, in accordance with the different characteristics of rich and poor, began to arise. The rich, for their part, had scarcely become acquainted with the pleasure of domination, before they soon disdained all others, and, using their former slaves to subdue new ones, they thought of nothing but subjugating and enslaving their neighbors, like those starving wolves that, having once tasted human flesh, rebuff all other food, and no longer want anything but to devour men.

In this way, since the most powerful or the most miserable made of their strength or their needs a kind of right to the possessions of others, equivalent, in their opinion, to the right of property, the destruction of equality was followed by the most frightful disorder. In this way, the usurpations of the rich, the brigandage of the poor, the unbridled passions of all, stifling natural compassion and the still feeble voice of justice, made men miserly, ambitious, and wicked. Between the right of the strongest and the right of the first occupant arose a perpetual conflict that ended only in fights and murders. Nascent society made way for the most horrible state of war; the human race, debased and desolate, no longer able to retrace its steps or give up the unfortunate acquisitions it had made, and working only toward its shame by abusing the faculties that honor it, brought itself to the brink of ruin.

*Attonitus novitate mali, divesque miserque,*
*Effugere optat opes, et quae modo voverat, odit.*°

It is impossible that men did not at last reflect upon such a miserable situation and upon the calamities that overwhelmed them. The rich, above all, must soon have felt how disadvantageous it was for them to have a state of perpetual war, in which they alone bore all the costs and in which the risk to life was common to all and that to property was specific to them. Furthermore, however they might color their usurpations, the rich sensed well enough that they were established only upon a precarious and abusive right, and that, since they were acquired only by force, force could take them away without their having any reason to complain about it. Even those whom ingenuity alone had made rich could scarcely base their ownership on better titles. They might well say: "I am the one who built this wall; I earned this land through my labor." Others could respond to them: "Who gave you the boundary lines; and on what basis do you claim the right to be paid at our expense for work we did not impose upon you? Are you unaware that many of your brothers perish or suffer from need of what you have in excess, and that you needed the express and unanimous consent of the human race to appropriate anything from the common subsistence that went beyond your own?" Lacking valid reasons to justify himself and strength sufficient to defend himself, easily crushing an individual but crushed himself by gangs of bandits, alone against all, and, on account of mutual jealousies, unable to unite with his equals against enemies united by the common hope of plunder, the rich man, pressed by necessity, finally conceived the most well-thought-out plan that ever entered the human mind; this was to use in his favor the very strength of those who were attacking him, to make his adversaries into his defenders, to appeal to them with other maxims and to give them other institutions that were as favorable to him as natural right was opposed.

To this end, after having explained to his neighbors the horror of a situation that armed them all against each other, that made their possessions as burdensome as their needs, and in which no one found safety either in poverty or in wealth, he easily invented specious reasons for leading them to his goal. "Let us unite," he says to them, "to protect the weak from oppression, to restrain the ambitious, and to assure each of the possession of what belongs to him: Let us institute rules of justice and peace with which all are bound to comply, which show no partiality, and which in some way compensate for the caprices of fortune by subjecting equally the powerful and the weak to mutual duties. In a word, instead of turning our forces against ourselves, let us gather them into a supreme power that governs us according to wise laws, protects and defends all the members of the association, repels common enemies, and maintains us in eternal concord."

Far less than the equivalent of this discourse was needed to win over crude, easily seduced men who had far too many matters to sort out among themselves to be able to do without arbitrators and too much avarice and ambition to be able for long to do without masters. All ran headlong into their chains, in the belief that they were securing their liberty, for, along with having reason enough to be conscious of the advantages of a political institution, they did not have enough experience to foresee its dangers; those most capable of anticipating the abuses were precisely those who counted on profiting from them, and even the wise saw the necessity of resolving to sacrifice one part of their liberty to preserve the other, just as a wounded man has his arm cut off to save the rest of his body.

Such was, or must have been, the origin of society and laws, which gave new fetters to the weak and new powers to the rich, irretrievably destroyed natural liberty, established forever the law of property and of inequality, made clever usurpation into an irrevocable right, and, for the benefit of an ambitious few, henceforth subjected the whole human race to labor, servitude, and misery.° It is easy to see how the establishment of a single society rendered that of all the others indispensable, and how, to face united forces, it was necessary to unite in turn. Societies, multiplying or spreading rapidly, soon covered the entire surface of the earth, and it was no longer possible to find a single corner in the universe where a person could throw off the yoke and pull his head out from under the often ill-guided sword he saw hanging perpetually over it. Once civil law had thus become the common rule of citizens, the law of nature retained a place only among the various societies, where, under the name of the law of nations, it was tempered by a few tacit conventions in order to make relations possible and to compensate for natural compassion, which, losing between one society and another nearly all the power that it had between one man and another, no longer resides in any but a few great cosmopolitan souls, who break through the imaginary barriers that separate peoples, and who, after the example of the sovereign being who created them, embrace the whole human race in their benevolence.

Remaining thus in the state of nature with each other, political bodies soon felt the effects of the disadvantages that had forced individuals to leave it, and this state became still more deadly among these great bodies than it had been formerly among the individuals of whom they were composed. Hence arose national wars, battles, murders, reprisals that make nature shudder and shock reason, and all those horrible prejudices that place the honor of shedding human blood in the ranks of the virtues. The most decent people learned to count among their duties that of slaughtering their fellow men; men were finally seen massacring each other by the thousands without knowing why; and more murders were committed in a single day of combat and more horrors in the storming of a single town, than had been committed in the state of nature during entire centuries over the whole face of the earth. Such are the first effects one glimpses of the division of the human race into different societies. Let us come back to their beginnings.

I know that several have ascribed other origins to political societies, such as the conquests of the most powerful, or the union of the weak, and the choice among these causes is immaterial to what I wish to establish. Nevertheless, the one I have just set forth seems to me the most natural for the following reasons. (1) Because, in the first case, since the right of conquest is not a right and could not be the basis of any other, the conquerer and the conquered peoples always remain in a state of war with each other, unless the nation, restored to complete freedom, voluntarily chooses its conqueror as its leader. Until then, whatever capitulations may have been made, since they have been founded only upon violence, and, consequently, since they are by this very fact null and void, there can be, in this hypothesis, neither true society nor body politic, nor any other law than that of the strongest. (2) Because, in the second case, these words *strong* and *weak* are equivocal, for, in the interval found between the establishment of the right of property or of first occupancy and that of political governments, the meaning of these terms is better rendered by the words *poor* and *rich*; because, before the laws, a man, in fact, had no other means of subjugating his equals than by attacking their property or by giving them some part of his own. (3) Because, since the poor had nothing to lose but their liberty, it would have been great folly for them to strip themselves voluntarily of the only good that remained to them only to gain nothing in exchange; because, since the rich were, on the contrary, vulnerable, so to speak, in every part of their wealth, it was much easier to do them harm, and they consequently had to take more precautions in order to protect themselves; and because, in short, it is reasonable to believe that a thing has been invented by those to whom it is useful rather than by those whom it wrongs.

Nascent government had no constant and regular form. The lack of philosophy and experience only allowed the perception of present disadvantages, and people thought of finding remedies for the others only as they appeared. Despite all the work of the wisest legislators, the political state always remained imperfect, because it was virtually the handiwork of chance, and since it was poorly begun, time, in revealing its flaws and suggesting remedies, could never repair the defects in the constitution. They continually patched it up, instead of beginning as would have been necessary by clearing the area and discarding all the old materials, just as Lycurgus did in Sparta, in order afterwards to raise a good structure. At first, society only consisted of a few general conventions that all private individuals promised to observe, and of which the community became guarantor for each one of them. Experience had to show how weak such a constitution was and how easy it was for offenders to avoid conviction or punishment for offenses of which the public alone was to be witness and judge; the law had to be evaded in a thousand ways; disadvantages and disorders had to multiply continually for people finally to think of confiding to individuals the dangerous trust of public authority and of committing to magistrates the task of upholding the decisions of the people, for to say that leaders were chosen before the confederation was formed and that ministers of the laws existed before the laws themselves is an assumption that may not be seriously debated.

It would be no more reasonable to believe that peoples first threw themselves, unconditionally and without hope of return, into the arms of an absolute master, and that the first means of providing for the common security devised by proud and untamed men was to rush headlong into slavery. Why indeed did they give themselves superiors if it was not to defend themselves against oppression and to protect their possessions, their liberties, and their lives, which are, so to speak, the constituent elements of their being? Now, in relations between one man and another, since the worst that can happen to one man is to find himself at the other's mercy, would it not have been contrary to common sense to begin by transferring into the hands of a leader the only things they needed his help to preserve? What equivalent could he have offered them for the concession of so precious a right, and, if he had dared to require it under the pretext of defending them, would he not immediately have received the response of the fable: "What more will the enemy do to us?" It is therefore incontestable, and it is the fundamental maxim of all political right, that peoples have given themselves leaders to protect their liberty and not to enslave themselves. "If we have a prince," said Pliny to Trajan, "it is so that he may preserve us from having a master."°

Political theorists engage in the same sophistry about the love of liberty as philosophers do about the state of nature; by things they see, they judge very different things they have not seen, and they attribute to men a natural inclination to servitude by the patience with which those they have before their eyes endure theirs, without thinking that it is the same for liberty as for innocence and virtue, the value of which is felt only insofar as one enjoys them himself, and the taste for which is lost as soon as one has lost them. "I know the delights of your country," Brasidas used to say to a satrap who was comparing life in Sparta to that in Persepolis, "but you cannot know the pleasures of mine."

Just as an untamed charger bristles, paws the ground with his hoof, and struggles impetuously at the mere approach of the bit, while a broken horse patiently suffers even the crop and spur, so savage man will not bow his head to the yoke that civilized man bears without a murmur, and he prefers the stormiest liberty to a tranquil subjugation. Man's natural disposition for or against servitude must not, therefore, be judged by the degradation of enslaved peoples, but by the wonders that all free peoples have wrought to save themselves from oppression. I know that the former do nothing but constantly praise the peace and repose they enjoy in their chains, and that *miserrimam servitutem pacem appellant.*° But when I see the others sacrificing pleasures, repose, wealth, power, and life itself for the preservation of this sole good, so despised by those who have lost it; when I see animals born free and abhorring captivity smash their heads against the bars of their prison; when I see multitudes of stark naked savages scorn European pleasures and brave hunger, fire, the sword, and death merely to preserve their independence, I sense that it is not for slaves to think about liberty.

As for paternal authority, from which several writers have derived absolute government and all society, it suffices to note, without taking recourse to the contrary proofs of Locke and Sidney, that nothing in the world is further from the ferocious spirit of despotism than the gentleness of that authority which looks more to the advantage of the one who obeys than to the benefit of the one who commands; that by the law of nature, the father is master of the child only as long as the child needs his help; that beyond this point they become equals; and that the son, perfectly independent of the father, then owes him only respect and not obedience, for gratitude is clearly a duty that should be repaid, but not a right that can be demanded. Instead of saying that civil society derives from paternal power, it should have been said, on the contrary, that this power draws its principal strength from civil society. An individual was acknowledged the father of several only as long as they remained assembled around him; the father's possessions, of which he is truly the master, are the bonds which keep the children dependent upon him, and he can give them a share in his estate only insofar as they clearly will have earned it by their constant deference to his wishes. Now, subjects are far from having some similar favor to expect from their despot, since they belong to him in their own right, they and all they possess, or at least he claims this to be the case; and they are reduced to receive as a favor whatever he leaves them of their own possessions: He gives justice when he robs them; he gives grace when he allows them to live.

By continuing in this way to examine facts in relation to right, we would find no more solidity than truth in the idea of a voluntary establishment of tyranny; and it would be difficult to show the validity of a contract that would be binding on only one of the parties, in which everything would be put on one side and nothing on the other, and which would tend only to harm the one who commits himself. This odious system is, even today, very far from being that of wise and good monarchs, and especially of the kings of France, as can be seen in various places in their edicts and particularly in the following passage from a famous document, published in 1667 in the name and by the orders of Louis XIV. *Let it not be said, therefore, that the sovereign is not subject to the laws of his state, since the contrary proposition is a truth of the law of nations, which flattery has sometimes attacked, but which good princes have always defended, as a tutelary divinity of their states. How much more legitimate it is to say with the wise Plato that perfect happiness in a kingdom is for a prince to be obeyed by his subjects, for the prince to obey the law, and for the law to be sound and always directed to the public good.*° I shall not stop to inquire into whether, since liberty is the noblest of man's faculties, he degrades his nature, puts himself on the level of beasts, slaves of instinct, and offends even the Author of his being by renouncing without reservation the most precious of all his gifts by agreeing to commit all the crimes He has forbidden to us in order to please a savage or insane master, nor whether this sublime craftsman would be more annoyed to see his finest handiwork destroyed than to see it dishonored. I shall disregard, if you wish, the authority of Barbeyrac, who clearly declares, following Locke, that no one can sell his liberty to the point of submitting to an arbitrary power that treats him according to its fancy. "*For,*" he adds, "*this would be to sell his own life, of which he is not the master.*"° I shall ask only by what right those who did not fear debasing themselves to this degree could subject their posterity to the same ignominy and renounce on its behalf assets that it does not owe to their liberality and without which life itself is burdensome to all who are worthy of it.

Pufendorf says that just as one transfers his property to another by agreements and contracts, he can also divest himself of his liberty in someone else's favor. This, it seems to me, is a very bad argument, for, in the first place, the property I alienate becomes something entirely foreign to me, and its abuse is immaterial to me, but it does matter to me that my liberty is not abused, and I cannot, without making myself guilty of the evil I shall be forced to do, leave myself open to becoming the instrument of crime. Moreover, since the right of property is only a matter of convention and human institution, every man can dispose of what he possesses as he pleases, but it is not the same for the essential gifts of nature, such as life and liberty, which everyone is permitted to enjoy and of which, it is at least doubtful that one has the right to divest oneself. By stripping himself of the one, a person degrades his being; by stripping himself of the other, he destroys it insofar as he can; and since no temporal good can compensate for either one, it would be an offense against both nature and reason to renounce them at any price whatsoever. But even if liberty could be given up like property, the difference would be very great for the children, who only enjoy the father's property by transmission of his right, since liberty is, instead, a gift that they derive from nature as men, of which their parents had no right to rob them. Thus, just as it was necessary to do violence to nature to establish slavery, so it was necessary to change nature to perpetuate this right; and the jurists who have gravely pronounced that the child of a slave would be born a slave have, in other words, decided that a man would not be born a man.

It appears certain to me, therefore, not only that governments did not have their beginnings in arbitrary power, which is only their corruption, their extreme limit, and which finally brings them back to the law of the strongest alone, for which they were at first the remedy, but also that, even if they had begun in that way, this power, being illegitimate by its nature, could not have served as a foundation for the laws of society, nor, consequently, for institutional inequality.

Without entering presently into the research that is yet to be done upon the nature of the fundamental pact of any government, I limit myself, in following common opinion, to considering here the establishment of the body politic as a true contract between the people and the leaders that it chooses for itself, a contract by which the two parties obligate themselves to observe laws that are stipulated in it and that form the bonds of their union. Since the people, with respect to social relations, have united all their wills into a single one, all the articles by which this will is explained become so many fundamental laws that bind all the members of the state without exception, and one of these regulates the choice and power of the magistrates charged with watching over the execution of the others. This power extends to everything that can maintain the constitution, without going so far as to change it. To it are joined honors that make the laws and their ministers respectable, and, for the latter personally, prerogatives that compensate them for the hard work needed for a good administration. The magistrate, for his part, is bound to use the power entrusted to him only in accordance with the intention of his constituents, to maintain each person in the peaceful enjoyment of what belongs to him, and to prefer on every occasion the public utility to his own interest.

Before experience had shown or knowledge of the human heart had made it possible to foresee the inevitable abuses of such a constitution, it must have seemed all the better, because those who were charged with seeing to its preservation were themselves most interested in it, for since magistracy and its rights are established only upon the fundamental laws, as soon as these were destroyed, magistrates would cease to be legitimate; the people would no longer be bound to obey them; and, since it would not have been the magistrates but the laws that had constituted the essence of the state, everyone would by right recover his natural liberty.

Provided that we reflect upon it attentively, this would be confirmed for new reasons, and by the nature of the contract, we would see that it could not be irrevocable, for, if there were no superior power that could guarantee the fidelity of the contracting parties or force them to fulfill their reciprocal commitments, the parties would remain sole judges in their own case, and each of them would always have the right to renounce the contract, as soon as he found that the other was violating its terms or that they had ceased to suit him. It seems that the right to abdicate may be founded upon this principle. Now, to consider, as we are doing, only what is instituted by man, if the magistrate, who has all the power in his hands and who appropriates to himself all the advantages of the contract, still had the right to renounce authority, the people, who pay

for all the leaders' mistakes, should with all the more reason, have the right to renounce their dependence. But the
dreadful dissensions, the endless disorders to which
this dangerous power would necessarily lead, show
more than anything else how greatly human governments
needed a basis more solid than reason alone, and how necessary it was to public tranquility for divine will to inter-
vene in order to give to sovereign authority a sacred and
inviolable character, which took away from the subjects
the fatal right to dispose of it. Even if religion had done
only this good for men, it would be enough to oblige them
all to cherish and adopt it, even with its abuses, since it
spares even more blood than fanaticism has shed. But let
us follow the thread of our hypothesis.

The various forms of governments have their origins
in the greater or lesser differences that existed among private individuals at the moment of their institution. If one
man was eminent in power, virtue, wealth, or esteem, he
alone was elected magistrate, and the state became monar-
chical; if several men equal among themselves in most
respects prevailed over all the others, they were jointly
elected, and there was an aristocracy; those whose fortunes or talents were less disproportionate and who
were least removed from the state of nature held the
supreme administration in common and formed a
democracy. Time confirmed which of these forms was
most advantageous to men. Some remained subject solely
to the laws; others soon obeyed masters. Citizens wanted
to protect their liberty; subjects thought only of taking it
away from their neighbors, finding it painful when others
are enjoying a good they no longer enjoyed themselves.
In a word, on one side were riches and conquests, and on
the other happiness and virtue.

In these different governments, all magistracies were
at first elective, and when wealth did not prevail, preference
was accorded to merit, which produces natural ascendency,

and to age, which produces experience in business and composure in deliberations. The elders of the Hebrews, the gerontes of Sparta, the senate of Rome, and the very etymology of our word *seigneur* show how greatly old age used to be respected. The more often elections fell upon men of advanced age, the more frequent they became, and the more their difficulties became apparent; intrigues were introduced, factions were formed, parties became embittered, civil wars were kindled; the blood of citizens was finally sacrificed to the so-called happiness of the state, and the people were on the verge of sinking back into the anarchy of earlier times. The ambition of the leaders profited from these circumstances to perpetuate their offices within their families; the people, already accustomed to dependence, tranquility, and the conveniences of life, and already incapable of breaking their chains, consented to allow their servitude to increase in order to strengthen their tranquility, and that is how the leaders, having become hereditary, became accustomed to regarding their magistracy as a family possession, and to regarding themselves as proprietors of the state of which they were at first only the officers; to calling their fellow citizens their slaves; to counting them like cattle among the things that belonged to them; and to calling themselves the equals of the gods and kings of kings.

If we follow the progress of inequality in these various revolutions, we shall find that the establishment of law and the right of property was its first stage, the institution of magistracy the second, and the third and last was the transformation of legitimate power into arbitrary power. Just so, the condition of rich and poor was authorized by the first epoch; that of powerful and weak by the second; and, by the third, that of master and slave, which is the final degree of inequality and the stage to which all the others lead, until new revolutions dissolve the government entirely or bring it closer to its legitimate institution.

To understand the necessity of this progress, we must give less consideration to the motives for the establishment of the body politic than to the form it takes in its implementation and to the disadvantages it entails, for the vices that make social institutions necessary are the same ones that make their abuse inevitable; and with the sole exception of Sparta, where laws primarily attended to the education of children, and where Lycurgus established moral habits that almost dispensed with the need for adding laws, the laws, generally weaker than the passions, restrain men without changing them; it would, therefore, be easy to prove that any government, which, without becoming corrupted or impaired, always functions exactly according to the aim of its founding would have been established unnecessarily, and that a country where no one evaded the laws and abused the magistracy would need neither laws nor magistrates.

Political distinctions necessarily lead to civil distinctions. The growing inequality between the people and its leaders soon makes itself felt among private individuals, and there it is modified in a thousand ways according to passions, talents, and circumstances. The magistrate cannot usurp illegitimate power without creating his own creatures to whom he is forced to yield some part of it. Besides, citizens allow themselves to be oppressed only as far as they are carried away by blind ambition, and looking more below than above themselves, domination becomes dearer to them than independence, and they consent to wear chains so that they can in turn give them to others. It is very difficult to reduce to obedience anyone who does not seek to command, and the most adroit politician would never succeed in subjugating men who wanted only to be free, but inequality spreads easily among ambitious and cowardly souls, always ready to run the risks of fortune and to dominate or serve almost indiscriminately, depending on whether fortune is favorable or unfavorable to them. Thus, a time must have come when the eyes of the people were beguiled to such a degree that its leaders had only to say to the least of men: "Be great, you and all your line," and he immediately appeared great to everyone as well as in his own eyes, and his descendants rose even higher the further they were removed from him; the more remote and uncertain the cause, the more the effect increased; the more idlers one could count in a family, the more illustrious it became.

If this were the place to go into detail, I would easily explain how, even without the involvement of government, inequality of recognition and authority becomes inevitable among private individuals[4] as soon as, united in the same society, they are forced to compare themselves to each other, and to take into account the differences that they find in the continual use they have to make of each other. These differences are of several kinds, but, in general, since wealth, nobility or rank, power, and personal merit are the principal distinctions by which we measure ourselves in society, I would demonstrate that the harmony or conflict of these different forces is the surest indication of a well- or poorly-constituted state; I would show that since among these four kinds of inequality, personal qualities are the origin of all the others, wealth is the one to which they are all reduced in the end, because being the most immediately useful to well-being and the easiest to pass on, it is easily used to purchase all the rest: An observation that makes it possible to assess rather exactly the extent to which each people is removed from its original institution and the progress it has made toward the furthest limits of corruption. I would observe how this universal desire for reputation, honors, and preferences, which consumes us all, trains and compares talents and strengths; how it excites and multiplies the passions; and how, by making all men competitors, rivals, or, rather, enemies, it daily causes setbacks, successes, and disasters of all kinds, by making so many contenders run in the same race. I would show that it is to this zeal for being talked about, to this frenzy to distinguish ourselves, that almost always keeps us outside ourselves, that we owe what is best and worst among men—our virtues and our vices, our sciences and our errors, our conquerors and our philosophers—that is to say, a multitude of bad things as compared to a few good ones. Finally, I would prove that if we see a handful of powerful and rich men at the pinnacle of greatness and fortune, while the crowd grovels in obscurity and misery, it is because the former value the things they enjoy only insofar as others are deprived of them, and because, without any change in their condition, they would cease being happy if the people ceased being miserable.

But these details alone would furnish the material for a lengthy work in which one would weigh the advantages and disadvantages of every government in relation to the rights of the state of nature, and where one would unmask all the different faces beneath which inequality has appeared up to this day and may appear in future centuries, according to the nature of those governments and the revolutions that time will necessarily bring about. We would see the multitude oppressed from within by the very precautions it had taken against what menaced it from without; we would see oppression continually growing without the oppressed ever being able to know what end it might have or what legitimate means would be left for them to stop it. We would see the rights of citizens and national liberties dying out little by little, and the complaints of the weak treated as seditious murmurs. We would see politics restricting the honor of defending the common cause to a mercenary segment of the people; we would see the necessity of taxes arising from this and the disheartened farmer quitting his field even during peacetime, leaving his plow to gird on the sword. We would see the birth of the bizarre and deadly rules of the code of honor; we would see the defenders of the homeland sooner or later become its enemies, constantly holding the dagger raised over their fellow citizens; and there would come a time when we would hear them saying to the oppressor of their country:

> *Pectore si fratris gladium juguloque parentis*
> *Condere me jubeas, gravidaeque in viscera partu*
> *Conjugis, invitâ peragam tamen omnia dextra.*°

From the extreme inequality of conditions and fortunes, from the diversity of passions and talents, from useless arts, from pernicious arts, from frivolous sciences would emerge a host of prejudices, equally contrary to reason, happiness, and virtue; we would see leaders stirring up everything that can weaken men gathered together by disuniting them; everything that can give society an air of apparent harmony and sow in it seeds of real division; everything that can inspire mistrust and mutual hatred in the different orders through the opposition of their rights and interests, and, consequently, fortifying the power that contains them all.

It is from the midst of this disorder and these uprisings that despotism, gradually raising its hideous head and devouring all that it had seen of the good and sound in every part of the state, would finally succeed in trampling the laws and the people underfoot and in establishing itself upon the ruins of the republic. The times that would precede this last change would be times of trouble and calamities, but, in the end, everything would be swallowed up by the monster, and peoples would no longer have leaders or laws, but only tyrants. From this moment, too, it would cease to be a matter of morality and virtue, for wherever despotism reigns, *cui ex honesto nulla est spes*;° it suffers no other master; as soon as it speaks, there is neither integrity nor duty to consult, and the blindest obedience is the only virtue left to slaves.

Here is the final stage of inequality and the extreme point that closes the circle and touches the point from which we set out. Here, all individuals become equals once again, because they are nothing, and once subjects have no law other than the will of the master and the master no other rule than his passions, notions of good and principles of justice vanish once more. It is here that everything comes down to the law of the strongest alone, and, consequently, to a new state of nature different from the one with which we began insofar as the first was the pure state of nature and the last is the fruit of excessive corruption. Besides, there is so little difference between these two states, and the contract of government is so completely dissolved by despotism that the despot is master only as long as he is the strongest, and, as soon as he can be driven out, he has no ground for protesting against the violence. The riot which ends with the strangling or dethroning of a sultan is as legal an act as those by which, the day before, he disposed of the lives and property of his subjects. Force alone maintained him; force alone overthrows him. Thus, all things happen in accordance with the natural order, and whatever the outcome of these short and frequent revolutions may be, no one can complain of the injustice of others, but only of his own imprudence or his misfortune.

By discovering and following, in this way, the forgotten and lost paths that must have led man from the natural to the civil state, by reestablishing, along with the intermediate positions I have just marked out, those which the pressures of time have made me suppress or which imagination has not suggested to me, any attentive reader can only be struck by the vast space that separates these two states. In this slow succession of things, he will see the solution to an endless number of moral and political problems that the philosophers cannot resolve. He will sense that since the human race of one age is not the human race of another age, the reason Diogenes found no human being was that he sought among his contemporaries the human being of a time that no longer existed. Cato, he will say, perished with Rome and liberty, because he was out of place in his times, and the greatest of men only astonished a world he would have governed five hundred years earlier. In short, he will explain how the soul and human passions, deteriorating imperceptibly, change in nature, so to speak; why the objects of our needs and pleasures change in the long run; why with the original man vanishing by degrees, society offers nothing more to the sage's eyes than an assemblage of unnatural men and artificial passions which are the handiwork of all these new relations and have no real foundation in nature. What reflection teaches us about that, observation confirms perfectly: savage man and civilized man differ so much in the depths of their hearts and their inclinations that what constitutes the supreme happiness of the one would reduce the other to despair. The former breathes only peace and liberty; he wants only to live and to remain idle, and not even the Stoic's ataraxia comes near his profound indifference to every other object. On the contrary, the always active citizen constantly sweats, agitates himself, torments himself to seek out still more laborious occupations. He works right up to the point of death; he even runs toward it to enable himself to live, or he renounces life to acquire immortality. He pays court to the great whom he hates and to the wealthy whom he despises; he spares nothing to gain the honor of serving them; he proudly boasts of his own baseness and of their protection, and, proud of his slavery, he speaks with disdain of those who do not have the honor of sharing it. What a spectacle for a Carib is the arduous and coveted work of a European minister! How many cruel deaths would this indolent savage not prefer to the horrors of such a life, which is often not even tempered by the pleasure of doing good? But for him to see the purpose of so many concerns, the words *power* and *reputation* would have to have some meaning in his mind, and he would have to learn that there is a sort of man who sets some value upon how the rest of the world looks at him, and who knows how to be happy and content with himself on the testimony of others rather than on his own. Such is, in fact, the real cause of all these differences: savage man lives within himself; social man, always outside of himself, knows only how to live in the opinion of others, and it is, so to speak, from their judgment alone that he derives the sentiment of his own existence. It is not my topic to show how, out of such a disposition, so much indifference toward good and evil arises, along with such fine moralistic discourses; how, once everything is reduced to appearances, all becomes artificial and feigned—honor, friendship, and virtue, and often even the vices which men finally discover the secret of boasting about; how, in a word, always asking others what we are and never daring to question ourselves about these matters in the midst of so much philosophy, humanity, civility, and so many sublime maxims, we have only a deceptive and frivolous exterior, honor without virtue, reason without wisdom, and pleasure without happiness. It suffices for me to have proved that this is not the original state of man, and that it is only the spirit of society and the inequality it engenders that in this way change and impair all our natural inclinations.

I have endeavored to lay out the origin and progress of inequality, the establishment and abuse of political societies, insofar as these things can be deduced from the nature of man by the light of reason alone and independently of the sacred dogmas which give to sovereign authority the sanction of divine right. It follows from this presentation that inequality, being almost nonexistent in the state of nature, derives its strength and growth from the development of our faculties and the progress of the human mind and finally becomes stable and legitimate through the establishment of property and laws. It follows, once again, that moral inequality, authorized by positive law alone, is contrary to natural right whenever it is not combined in the same proportion with physical inequality, a distinction that adequately determines what should be thought in this regard about the kind of inequality that is prevalent among all civilized peoples, since it is manifestly contrary to the law of nature, however we define it, for a child to command an old man, for a fool to lead a wise man, and for a handful of people to abound in superfluities, while the starving multitude lacks the bare necessities.

# Rousseau's Notes to the 1755 Edition

1. **[Note IX]** A famous author, calculating the good and ills in human life and comparing the two sums, found that the latter surpassed the former by far, and that, all things considered, life was, for man, a rather poor gift. I am not surprised by his conclusion; he has taken all his arguments from the constitution of civil man. If he had gone back to natural man, one can judge that he would have obtained very different results, that he would have seen that man has scarcely any ills other than those he has given himself, and that nature would have been justified. It is not without difficulty that we have succeeded in making ourselves so unhappy. When we consider, on the one hand, the vast labors of men, the many sciences thoroughly developed, the many arts invented, so many forces utilized, chasms filled, mountains razed, rocks broken up, rivers made navigable, lands cleared, lakes dug out, swamps drained, enormous buildings raised on earth, seas covered with ships and sailors; and when we inquire, on the other, with a little meditation about the real advantages that have resulted from all that for the happiness of the human species, we can only be struck by the astonishing disproportion that reigns among these things and deplore the blindness of man, who, in order to feed his foolish pride and I know not what vain admiration for himself, runs

eagerly after all the miseries to which he is susceptible, and from which beneficent nature had taken care to keep him.

Men are wicked—sad and continual experience dispenses with the need for proof; I believe, however, that I have demonstrated that man is naturally good. What, therefore, can have depraved him to this extent, if not the changes that have arisen in his constitution, the progress he has made, and the knowledge that he has acquired? Let us admire human society as much as we wish; it will be no less true that it necessarily brings men to hate each other to the degree that their interests conflict, to render to each other apparent services, and, in fact, to do every imaginable harm to each other. What can be thought of dealings in which the reason of each private individual dictates maxims to him directly contrary to those that public reason preaches to the body of society, and in which each finds his profit in the misfortune of others? There is perhaps no well-to-do man whose avid heirs, and often his own children, do not secretly wish for his death; no ship at sea whose sinking would not be good news to some merchant; no firm that a dishonest debtor would not like to see burned along with all the papers it contains; no people that does not rejoice in the disasters of its neighbors. In this way, we find our advantage in the losses of our fellow men, and that one person's ruin almost always creates another's prosperity, but what is still more dangerous is that public calamities become the expectation and hope of a great many private individuals. Some wish for illnesses, others for death, others for war, others for famine; I have seen dreadful men weep with sorrow at the prospect of a fertile year, and the great and deadly fire of London, which cost the lives or property of so many unfortunates, made the fortune of perhaps more than ten thousand persons. I know that Montaigne blames the Athenian Demades for having had a worker punished who, by selling coffins at a very high price, earned a great deal from the death of citizens. But, since Montaigne advances the argument that all of them should be punished, it evidently confirms my own.° Let us penetrate, therefore, through our frivolous displays of good will to what goes on in the depth of our hearts, and let us reflect upon what the state of things must be where all men are forced to cherish and destroy each other, and where they are born enemies by duty and deceivers by interest. If someone answers me that society is constituted in such a way that each man gains by serving others, I shall reply that this would be very well if he did not gain still more by harming them. There is no legitimate profit that is not surpassed by one that can be made illegitimately, and the wrong done to one's neighbor is always more lucrative than the good turns. It is, therefore, no longer a question of anything more than finding ways of being assured of impunity, and it is to this end that the powerful use all their strength and the weak all their cunning.

When he has eaten, savage man is at peace with all of nature and the friend of all his fellow men. If a dispute sometimes arises over his meal? He never comes to blows without first having compared the difficulty of winning with that of finding his sustenance elsewhere; and since pride is not involved in the combat, it ends with a few blows of the fist; the victor eats, the vanquished goes off to seek his fortune, and everyone is pacified. But for man in society, there are very different concerns; it is, in the first place, a question of providing for essentials and then for the luxuries; next come the delights, then immense riches, and then subjects and then slaves; he does not have a moment's respite. What is most peculiar is that the less natural and urgent his needs, the more his passions grow, and what is worse, the power to satisfy them, so that after lengthy prosperity, after having swallowed up many treasures and having tormented many men, my hero will end by slaughtering everything until he is the sole master of the universe. Such is, in brief, the moral picture, if not of human life, at least of the secret pretensions in the heart of every civilized man.

Compare without prejudice the condition of civil man with that of savage man, and search, if you can, the extent to which—beyond his wickedness, his needs, and his miseries—the former has opened new doors to pain and death. If you consider the sorrows of mind that consume us, the violent passions that exhaust and distress us, the excessive work with which the poor are overburdened, and the still more dangerous softness to which the rich abandon themselves, so that the former die from their needs and the latter from their excesses; if you think of the monstrous mixtures of foods, their pernicious seasonings, the tainted foodstuffs, the adulterated drugs, the knavery of those who sell them, the errors of those who administer them, the poison of the vessels in which they are prepared; if you pay attention to the epidemic diseases engendered by the bad air among throngs of men gathered together; to those caused by the delicacy of our way of living, going back and forth from inside our houses out into the fresh air; to the use of clothing put on or taken off with too little precaution; and to all the concerns that our excessive sensuality has turned into necessary habits which, if we neglect them or deprive ourselves of them, cost us our life or health; if you take into account the fires and earthquakes which, by burning or turning entire cities upside down, cause the inhabitants to perish by the thousands; in a word, if you bring together the dangers that all these causes continually gather over our heads, you will feel how dearly nature makes us pay for the contempt in which we have held its lessons.

I shall not repeat here what I have said elsewhere about war, but I wish knowledgeable people would want or dare just once to give the public details of the horrors that are committed in armies by the contractors for food supplies and hospitals; we would see that their not-too-secret maneuvers, by which even the most brilliant armies dissolve in no time at all, cause more soldiers to perish than are cut down by enemy swords; no less astonishing is the calculation of the number of men swallowed up every year by the sea, whether by hunger, scurvy, pirates, fire, or shipwrecks. It is clear we must also assign to established ownership, and, consequently, to society, assassinations, poisonings, highway robberies, and even the punishments for these crimes, punishments necessary to prevent greater evils, but which, for the murder of one man, costing the lives of two or more, continually double the real loss to the human species. How many shameful means of preventing the birth of men and outwitting nature are there? Either by those brutal and depraved tastes that insult its most charming handiwork, tastes that savages and animals never knew and that have arisen in civilized countries only in corrupt imaginations; or by those secret abortions, the worthy fruits of debauchery and perverted honor; or by the exposure or murder of a great many infants, victims of their parents' poverty or the barbarous shame of their mothers; or, finally, by the mutilation of those unfortunates, a part of whose existence and entire posterity are sacrificed to vain whims, or what is worse still, to the brutal jealousy of a few men, a mutilation that, in this last case, doubly outrages nature, both by the treatment received by those who suffer from it and by the use to which they are destined.

What if I undertook to show the human species attacked at its roots and even in the most holy of all bonds, where no one any longer dares to listen to nature except after having consulted fortune, and where, with civil disorder confusing virtues with vices, continence becomes a criminal precaution, and the refusal to grant one's fellow man his life an act of humanity? But without lifting the veil that covers up so many horrors, let us be content with identifying the evil for which others must supply the remedy.

To all that, let us add the scores of unhealthy trades that shorten one's days or destroy one's constitution, such as work in mines, the various preparations of metals and minerals, especially lead, copper, mercury, cobalt, arsenic, realgar, and those other perilous trades that daily cost the lives of scores of workers, some roofers, others carpenters, others masons, others working quarries; let us bring together all these things, I say, and we shall be able to see in the establishment and development of societies the reasons for the diminution of the species observed by more than one philosopher.

Luxury, impossible to prevent among men eager for their own conveniences and for the respect of others, soon completes the evil begun by societies, and under the pretext of supporting the poor, whom it need not have created, it impoverishes all the rest, and sooner or later depopulates the state.

Luxury is a remedy much worse than the evil it claims to cure; or rather, it is itself the worst of all the evils in any state, however large or small it may be, that, in order to provide for the throngs of valets and paupers it has created, devastates and ruins the plowman and the citizen, like those scorching south winds at midday that, covering the grass and greenery with voracious insects, deprive useful animals of their sustenance and carry famine and death into all the places where they are felt.

From society and from the luxury it engenders arise the liberal and mechanical arts, commerce, letters, and all these useless things that make human industry flourish, enrich and ruin states. The reason for this decay is very simple. It is easy to see that, by its nature, agriculture must be the least lucrative of all the arts, because, given that the use of its products is the most indispensable for all men, its price must be proportionate to the capabilities of the poorest. From the same principle we can derive the rule that, in general, the arts are lucrative in an inverse proportion to their utility and that the most necessary must finally become the most neglected. From this we see what must be thought of the true advantages of human industry and the actual effects that result from its progress.

Such are the perceptible causes of all the miseries into which opulence finally plunges the most admired nations. To the degree that industry and the arts spread and flourish, the scorned farmer, burdened by taxes necessary for the maintenance of luxury and condemned to spend his life between work and hunger, abandons his fields to seek in the cities the bread he should bring there. The more the capitals strike the stupid eyes of the people as admirable, the more necessary it is to moan at seeing the countryside abandoned, land uncultivated, and highways inundated with unfortunate citizens who have become beggars or thieves, destined one day to end their misery on the wheel or a dung heap. That is how the state, growing rich on one hand, grows weak and becomes depopulated on the other, and how the most powerful monarchies, after much labor to make themselves affluent and deserted, end by becoming the prey of poor nations that succumb to the deadly temptation to invade them and that, in turn, grow rich and weak, until they are themselves invaded and destroyed by others.

Let someone deign to explain to us just once what could have produced those hordes of barbarians who inundated Europe, Asia, and Africa for so many centuries. Was it to the vigor of their arts, to the wisdom of their laws, to the excellence of their organization that they owed this prodigious population? Let our scholars kindly tell us why, far from multiplying to this degree, these ferocious and brutal men, without knowledge, restraint, and education, did not all cut each other's throats at every moment in fighting for their pastures or hunting grounds. Let them explain to us how these wretched men even had the audacity to look straight into the eyes of people as clever as we were, with such fine military discipline, such fine codes, and such wise laws. Finally, why, since society has been developed most fully in the countries of the north, and since so much trouble has been taken there to teach men their mutual duties and the art of living together agreeably and peacefully, do we no longer see anything coming out like those multitudes of men that were produced in the past? I am very afraid that someone will at last dare to respond to me that all these great things, namely the arts, the sciences, and the laws, have been wisely invented by men as a salutary pestilence to prevent the excessive multiplication of the species, for fear that this world destined for us might in the end become too small for its inhabitants.

What then? Is it necessary to destroy societies, to annihilate yours and mine, and to return to living in the forests with the bears? An inference after the manner of my adversaries that I would rather anticipate than leave them with the shame of drawing it. O you, to whom the celestial voice has not made itself heard and who acknowledge no other destiny for your species than to reach the end of this short life in peace; you who can leave your fatal acquisitions, your anxious minds, your corrupt hearts, and your unbridled desires in the middle of cities, recapture—since it depends on you—your ancient and original innocence; go into the woods to lose the sight and memory of the crimes of your contemporaries and have no fear of demeaning your species by renouncing its knowledge in order to renounce its vices. As for men like me, whose passions have forever destroyed their original simplicity, who can no longer subsist on grass and acorns nor do without laws and leaders; those who were honored in their first father with supernatural lessons; those who will see, in the intention of giving to human actions in the beginning a morality they would have acquired over a long period of time, the reason for a precept that is unimportant in itself and inexplicable within every other system; those, in a word, who are convinced that the divine voice called the entire human race to the enlightenment and happiness of the celestial intelligences; all those will try, through the exercise of the virtues they force themselves to practice while learning to know them, to deserve the eternal reward they must expect from them; they will respect the sacred bonds of the societies of which they are members; they will love their fellow men and serve them with all their power; they will scrupulously obey the laws and the men who are their authors and ministers; they will honor above all the good and wise princes who will know how to prevent, cure, or palliate the host of abuses and evils always ready to overwhelm us; they will stir the zeal of these worthy chiefs by showing them without fear and flattery the magnitude of their task and the rigor of their duty. But they will have no less contempt for a constitution that can be maintained only with the help of so many respectable people who are more often wanted than found, and from which, despite all their care, always arise more real calamities than apparent advantages.°

2. [**Note XI**] That seems most obvious to me, and I cannot conceive how our philosophers can establish the origin of all those passions they attribute to natural man. Except for the bare physical necessities that nature itself demands, all our other needs have arisen only through habit, before which they were not needs, or through our desires, and one does not desire what one is not in a position to know. From this it follows that since savage man desires only the things he knows and knows only the things that he has the power to possess or that are easy to acquire, nothing could be as tranquil as his soul or as limited as his mind.

3. [**Note XV**] Self-love and love of self must not be confused, two very different passions by nature and in their effects. Love of self is a natural sentiment that inclines every animal to look after its own preservation and that, guided in man by reason and modified by compassion, produces humanity and virtue. Self-love is only a relative, artificial sentiment and born in society, one that leads each individual to place greater value on himself than on anyone else, that inspires in men all the evils they do to one another, and that is the true source of honor.

With this firmly in mind, I say that in our original state, in the true state of nature, self-love did not exist, for, since each man individually looks upon himself as the only witness who observes him, as the only being in the universe who takes an interest in him, as the only judge of his own merit, it is impossible for a sentiment that originates in comparisons he is not capable of making to germinate in his soul; for the same reason, this man has neither hate nor the desire for revenge, passions that can arise only from the opinion that one has been offended; and, since it is the contempt or the intention to do harm and not the wrong itself that constitutes the offense, men who know neither how to value each other nor how to compare themselves with each other can do a great deal of violence to each other, when they gain some advantage from it, without ever offending each other. In a word, each man, hardly seeing his fellow man except as he would see animals of another species, can steal prey from the weaker or give his up to the stronger, without viewing this pillaging as anything other than natural events, without the least surge of insolence or spite, and without any passion other than the sadness or joy of success or failure.°

4. **[Note XIX]** Distributive justice would itself oppose this rigorous equality of the state of nature, even if it were practicable in civil society, and since all members of the state owe it services proportionate to their talents and strengths, citizens must in turn be recognized and favored in proportion to their services. It is in this sense that we must understand a passage from Isocrates in which he praises the first Athenians for having known well how to distinguish which of the two kinds of equality was the more advantageous, of which one consisted in sharing the same advantages equally among all citizens, and the other in distributing them according to the merit of each. These skillful politicians, adds the orator, banishing that unjust equality that makes no distinction between wicked and good people, cling scrupulously to the one that rewards and punishes each according to his merit. But, in the first place, no society has ever existed, whatever degree of corruption they may have reached, in which no distinction was made between wicked and good people, and in the matter of moral habits, where the law cannot establish measures exact enough to serve as rules for the magistrate, it very wisely prohibits him from judging persons by allowing him to judge only actions, in order not to leave the fate or rank of citizens to his discretion. Only moral habits as pure as those of the ancient Romans could withstand censors, and similar tribunals would soon have wreaked havoc among

us. It is for public esteem to make the distinction between wicked and good men; the magistrate is the judge only of sound law, but the people is the true judge of moral habits; an honest and even enlightened judge on this issue, a judge that is occasionally fooled but never corrupted. The ranks of citizens must, therefore, be regulated, not on their personal merit, which would leave the magistrates with the means of applying the law in an almost arbitrary fashion, but on the actual services they render to the state, and that are open to a more accurate estimate.

# Notes

**p. 3** *Aristotle*, Politics, *I.5.1254a*: "We do not seek what is natural in depraved beings, but among those who comport themselves in conformity with nature."

**p. 5** *Preface*: We have omitted Rousseau's "Dedication to the Republic of Geneva." In it he praises Geneva as a free democracy despite the fact that it was an oligarchy at the time the *Discourse* was written. Readers disagree as to how to understand this discrepancy. Perhaps Rousseau was painting for Genevans a picture of what their city could and should become?

**p. 5** *the inscription on the temple at Delphi*: "Know thyself."

**p. 7** *in order to judge our own present condition properly*: Many readers of the *Discourse* have failed to take seriously Rousseau's statement here that he does not take his depiction of the original state of nature to be historically accurate and that such a state may never have existed.

**p. 8** *his constitution, and his condition*: Jean-Jacques Burlamaqui, *Principes du droit naturel*, 1747.

**p. 10** *two principles that are prior to reason . . . perish or suffer*: These are Rousseau's first characterizations of what he later calls love of self (*amour de soi-même*) and compassion, respectively.

**p. 12** *Quem te Deus esse / Jussit, et humana qua parte locatus es in re, / Disce*: Persius, *Satires*, III.71–73. "Learn what divinity has ordered you to be, and what your place is in human affairs."

PART I

**p. 20** *An illustrious philosopher*: Montesquieu, *The Spirit of the Laws*, I.2.

**p. 31** *the Abbé de Condillac*: Étienne Bonnot de Condillac, *Essay on the Origin of Human Knowledge.*

**p. 40** tanto plus in illis proficit vitiorum ignoratio, quam in his cognitio virtutis: Justin, *Histories*, II.ii.15. "Among them [the Scythians], ignorance of the vices has been much more profitable than knowledge of the virtues among those others [the Greeks]."

**p. 42** *self-love: amour propre.*

**p. 42** *love of self: amour de soi-même.*

PART 2

**p. 57** *the first step toward inequality and, at the same time, toward vice*: References to public esteem and the desire to be well regarded by others make clear that Rousseau is singling out self-love (*amour propre*) as the first step toward inequality.

**p. 58** *For, according to the axiom of the wise Locke,* there can be no injury, where there is no property: roughly cited from *An Essay Concerning Human Understanding*, IV.iii.18.

**p. 58** *self-love: amour propre.*

**p. 62** *self-love: amour propre.*

**p. 64** Attonitus novitate mali, divesque miserque, / Effugere optat opes, et quae modo voverat, odit: Ovid, *Metamorphoses*, XI.127–28. "Shocked by the newness of the ill, rich, and yet wretched, he seeks to run away from his wealth and hates what he once prayed for."

**p. 67** *subjected the whole human race to labor, servitude, and misery*: In *The Social Contract* Rousseau presents a vision of a legitimate republic aimed at solving the problems depicted in the present text.

**p. 70** *"If we have a prince," said Pliny to Trajan, "it is so that he may preserve us from having a master"*: Pliny the Younger (c. 61–114), *Panegyricus*, LV.7.

**p. 71** miserrimam servitutem pacem appellant: Tacitus (c. 55—c. 114), *Histories*, IV.xvii. "The most wretched servitude they call peace."

**p. 72** Let it not be said . . . always directed to the public good: Anonymous, *A Treatise on the Rights of the Most Christian Queen over Various States of the Spanish Monarchy.*

**p. 73** *"this would be to sell his own life, of which he is not the master"*: Samuel Pufendorf, *The Law of Nature and Nations,* VII.7.6, note 6, as translated by Jean Barbeyrac.

**p. 81** Pectore si fratris gladium juguloque parentis / . . . tamen omnia dextra: Lucan, *On the Civil War,* I.376–78. "If you order me to bury my sword in my brother's breast or my father's throat or my pregnant wife's belly, I will do it all, even if my right hand is unwilling."

**p. 81** cui ex honesto nulla est spes: Tacitus, *Annals,* V.iii. " . . . in which no hope is afforded by honesty."

## ROUSSEAU'S NOTES TO THE 1755 EDITION

**p. 88** *Montaigne advances the argument that all of them should be punished, it evidently confirms my own*: Michel de Montaigne, *Essays,* chapter XXI.

**p. 93** *always arise more real calamities than apparent advantages*: The final paragraph of Rousseau's note here is important, for he states clearly that he is not recommending a return to the original state of nature.

**p. 94** *without any passion other than the sadness or joy of success or failure*: In this important note Rousseau distinguishes two passions, each of which could be described as a kind of self-love. *Amour de soi-même,* translated here as "love of self," was defined earlier as a natural and benign interest in one's well-being and self-preservation (see note to p. 10). *Amour propre,* translated here as "self-love," is a concern for the esteem or recognition of others. It is a relative passion in two senses: it seeks the good *opinion of others*, and it seeks a recognized standing *in comparison to others*—which can include, as Rousseau emphasizes here, superior standing. Although in this text Rousseau emphasizes the dangers of *amour propre*, in *Emile* he allows that it can be formed through education so as to be part of a virtuous character.

# Further Reading

The secondary literature on Rousseau is vast and highly diverse. I provide here a very brief guide to further reading intended to encourage readers to explore some of the literature most relevant to a philosophical interpretation of the *Discourse on the Origin of Inequality*. No one can pretend to have the final word on any of Rousseau's texts, and many other secondary works are worth consulting as well.

Christopher Brooke, "Rousseau's Second Discourse: Between Epicureanism and Stoicism," in *Rousseau and Freedom*, eds Christie McDonald and Stanley Hoffmann (Cambridge: Cambridge University Press, 2010), 44–57.

Ernst Cassirer, *The Question of Jean-Jacques Rousseau*, trans. Peter Gay (New Haven, CT.: Yale University Press, 1989); reprinted in John T. Scott, *Jean-Jacques Rousseau: Critical Assessments*, 4 vols. (London: Routledge, 2006), vol. 1, 48–78.

Joshua Cohen, "The Natural Goodness of Humanity," in *Reclaiming the History of Ethics*, ed. Andrews Reath, Barbara Herman, and Christine M. Korsgaard (Cambridge: Cambridge University Press, 1997), 102–39.

Laurence D. Cooper, *Rousseau, Nature, and the Problem of the Good Life* (University Park: Pennsylvania State University Press, 1999).

N.J.H. Dent, *Rousseau: An Introduction to His Psychological, Social and Political Theory* (Oxford: Blackwell, 1988), chapters 1–3.

Victor Gourevitch, "Rousseau's Pure State of Nature," *Interpretation* 16 (Fall 1988): 23–59.

Christopher Kelly and Roger D. Masters, "Human Nature, Liberty and Progress: Rousseau's Dialogue with the Critics of the *Discours sur l'Inégalité*," in Scott, *Jean-Jacques Rousseau: Critical Assessments* (see above), 257–71.

Arthur O. Lovejoy, "The Supposed Primitivism of Rousseau's *Discourse on Inequality*," in A. O. Lovejoy, *Essays in the History of Ideas* (Baltimore: Johns Hopkins University Press, 1948); reprinted in Scott, *Jean-Jacques Rousseau: Critical Assessments* (see above), vol. 1, 29–47.

Arthur M. Melzer, *The Natural Goodness of Man* (Chicago: University of Chicago Press, 1990), parts 1–2.

Susan Neiman, "Metaphysics, Philosophy: Rousseau on the Problem of Evil," in *Reclaiming the History of Ethics*, ed. Reath, Herman, and Korsgaard (see above), 140–69.

Frederick Neuhouser, *Rousseau's Critique of Inequality: Reconstructing the Second Discourse* (Cambridge: Cambridge University Press, 2014).

Timothy O'Hagan, *Rousseau* (London: Routledge, 1999), chapter 2.

Marc F. Plattner, *Rousseau's State of Nature: An Interpretation of the Discourse on Inequality* (DeKalb: Northern Illinois University Press, 1979).

John T. Scott, "The Theodicy of the Second Discourse: The 'Pure State of Nature' and Rousseau's Political Thought," *American Political Science Review* 86 (September 1992): 696–711; reprinted in Scott, *Jean-Jacques Rousseau: Critical Assessments* (see above), vol. 2, 225–56.

## ABOUT THE NORTON LIBRARY

### Exciting texts you can't get anywhere else

The Norton Library is the only series that offers an inexpensive, student-friendly edition of Emily Wilson's groundbreaking version of Homer's *Odyssey*, or Carole Satyamurti's thrilling, prize-winning rendition of the *Mahabharata*, or Michael Palma's virtuoso *terza rima* translation of Dante's *Inferno*—to name just three of its unique offerings. Distinctive translations like these, exclusive to the Norton Library, are the cornerstone of the list, but even texts originally written in English offer unique distinctions. Where else, for instance, will you find an edition of John Stuart Mill's *Utilitarianism* edited and introduced by Peter Singer? Only in the Norton Library.

### The Norton touch

For more than 75 years, W. W. Norton has published texts that are edited with the needs of students in mind. Volumes in the Norton Library all offer editorial features that help students read with more understanding and pleasure—to encounter the world of the work on its own terms, but also to have a trusted travel guide navigate them through that world's unfamiliar territory.

### Easy to afford, a pleasure to own

Volumes in the Norton Library are inexpensive—among the most affordable texts available—but they are designed and produced with great care to be easy on the eyes, comfortable in the hand, and a pleasure to read and re-read over a lifetime.

**W. W. NORTON & COMPANY**
*Independent Publishers Since 1923*